C000283800

Exotic Garden Plants
in the
Channel Islands

Above: *Ensete* leaf

Front cover: *Cordyline, Canna, Musa* and *Yucca*
blend to give an exotic look to the garden,
author's own garden, Jersey

Back cover: Deep pink *Leptospermum scoparium*

Above: *Phormium* and *Lampranthus*, L'Etacq, Jersey
Opposite: A variety of exotics, including *Geranium maderensa* and *Echium fastuosum* outside White House Hotel, Herm

Exotic Garden Plants in the Channel Islands

Janine Le Pivert

SEAFLOWER BOOKS

Published in 2007 by Seaflower Books
16A St John's Road
St Helier
Jersey   JE2 3LD

Origination by Seaflower Books

Printed in Italy

ISBN 978-1- 903341-40-7

Acknowledgements
I would like to thank the following people for their invaluable help, advice and expertise:-
Martin and Christine Bourke, Mike de Carteret, Bernard and Margery Le Masurier, Nicky Stewart, Jean-Pierre Vaines and especially Ray and Annette Le Pivert. Extra special thanks to Bruce for his patience and for being there for me.

Photo Credits
I appreciate the opportunity, freely given by many people, to photograph plants in their own gardens. All the photographs in this book were taken by the author, Janine Le Pivert, with the following exceptions, for which I am very grateful:
Nicky Stewart: *Lavendula* p97 (all 3) *Zantesdechia* p110, Author's photo, back cover.
Bernard Le Masurier: *Geranium* p12, *Fascicularia* p35, *Phygelius* p99, *Crinum* p105.
Lesley Bailey: White House Hotel, p3, *Echium wildpretii* p29, *Furcraea* p35.
Ray Le Pivert: *Passiflora* p51 & p54, *Camellia* p118, *Pieris*, p120.
Garry Platt: *Astelia* p34, *Clianthus* p55, *Geranium* p94.
P M J de Carteret: *C.* 'Album' p113, *N. sarniensis* p109.
Serge Aubert: (Jardin Botanique Alpin du Lautaret, Grenoble University) *Eccremocarpus* p56.
Terry Blackburn: *Trachelospermum* p56.
Wayne Boucher: *Arctotis* p48.
Nigel Kembrey: *Butia* p21.
Owen Rogers: *Akebia* p55.
Robert Smith/Chapel Studios: La Seigneurie p117.

This book is dedicated to Natasha and Katherine

Contents

Symbols Guide

Plant Site		Soil Type		Hardiness	
Full sun	☀	Dry, well-drained	◌	Hardy above −15°C	❄
Partial shade	◐	Well-drained	◓	Hardy above −7°C	❄
Full shade	○	Moisture retentive	●	Hardy above −2°C	❄

Introduction

I decided to write this book to give Channel Islanders and visitors an idea of the plants that grow well locally, and how planting them can give their gardens the 'wow' factor that will make people stop and stare in amazement. Being Jersey born I was, perhaps, blasé about the wealth of exotic plants growing in the Channel Islands, unaware that this far north we are unusually blessed with a climate that allows the growth of an exceptional variety of plants.

A trip to Australia opened my eyes to their range of flamboyant shrubs, many of which I had seen equally at home in the Channel Islands. Lots of the plants that are so familiar to us, such as the wonderful blue globes of *Agapanthus*, the spiky *Cordyline* and even the Jersey and Guernsey lilies were once overseas visitors that decided to stay.

The Islands can support many plants that you would not expect to grow in Britain, ones that give a foreign, far-away feel and even further north, everyone can cultivate their own corner of paradise at home.

This effect doesn't need a whole garden full of exotica; even a single clump of hardy bananas, a specimen palm or tree fern will give your garden an exotic feel. If you pick the right location and give some extraordinary plants what they need within the limitations of your garden, you can then sit back and accept the neighbours' admiring glances! Whilst we can push the boundaries with elaborate winter protection against frost, wind and rain, this book demonstrates what will grow locally without all that extra work.

All the common plants in this book can be left outside with minimal protection, and usually none, here in the Channel Islands.

None of us likes running outside with armfuls of straw and fleece every time a cold snap is forecast, only to take it off again a few days later when it turns mild and wet. By all means, invest in one or two tender exotics and bring them into the conservatory or house for the winter. However, this book aims to give you guidelines on garden plants with that tropical look that have proven staying power in our usual winters, and that will pick up after the long winter to look great again without much effort from you.

Whilst this book does not have an exhaustive list of every possible exotic that we can grow, I have either grown, or seen growing in the Channel Islands, every one of the main plants listed. I have also seen many of the 'others worth trying' here too and I am sure that there are several unusual plants growing away merrily in the corner of some adventurous local gardener's plot!

I have also included information about the soil preferences, and, just as importantly, the hardiness of each plant as some of my readers may be visitors to our shores from cooler climates. You may well wish to try some of 'our' exotics on the mainland, and with climate change this could become easier to do, and, of course, many of the plants are much hardier than their appearance suggests.

We are so lucky to live in a climate that allows us to push the gardening boundaries far beyond what is expected from a latitude so far north and I encourage you all to give exotic gardening a go, then relax and enjoy your own personal oasis!

Janine Le Pivert
Jersey
April 2007

The Channel Islands

The archipelago of five main islands lies between the latitudes of 49° and 50° North in the Bay of Mont St. Michel, off the northern coast of France. The largest, and most populated, are Jersey and Guernsey. The other three are Alderney, Sark and Herm. Smaller islets include Brecqhou, Jethou, Lihou, Burhou and the rocky Minquiers and Ecrehous off the coasts of Jersey.

Jersey is the largest and most southerly of the Channel Islands. It is roughly rectangular in shape and measures approximately 10.8 miles east-west and 6.8 miles north-south. It is commonly spoken of as being 9 by 5 miles as the area is only 45 square miles due to irregularities in the coastline. The land slopes roughly from rugged cliffs in the north down to sandy beaches in the south and west, backed by wide coastal plains. Jersey's eastern edge is only 12 miles from the Normandy coast.

Guernsey is the second largest island, approximately 9 miles by 5 miles wide in a triangular shape covering 25 square miles in area. It is situated 30 miles west of France's Normandy coast and 75 miles south of Weymouth in England and is the most westerly of the Channel Islands. Guernsey has a high southern plateau, and a low-lying, and sandy, northern region.

Alderney is 20 miles north of Guernsey and the 2 by 3 mile island is the northernmost of the Channel Islands, only 8 miles from France and some 55 miles south of the English mainland. Alderney is similar to the other islands in that it has sheer cliffs broken by stretches of sandy beach and dunes.

Sark lies 9 miles to the south-east of Guernsey. It is small, at only 3 miles long by 1.5 miles wide, yet it has a coastline of 40 miles with steep cliff-backed coves and sheltered bays.

Herm is 3 miles off Guernsey's east coast. It is just 1.5 by 0.6 miles in size yet enjoys the varied terrain of the other islands with cliffs in the south and wide sandy beaches to the north.

The principal bedrock of the Islands is granite. As a result, the soil tends to be acidic, and can be poor on high land where the rock is close to the surface. Most of the soils of the interiors, however, are deep and well-drained and allow the growth of most varieties of plants. The coastal areas of the south and west in Jersey, north and west in Guernsey, and parts of the other islands have received considerable quantities of blown sand resulting in very light soils that can be high in lime because of broken-down mollusc shells. These sandy soils are exceptionally free draining and are ideal for many of the succulents discussed in this book.

The Local Climate

Climate Type

A noticeable theme throughout this book is that many of the exotic plants originate from parts of the world that have a specific climate type, i.e. what is known as a 'mediterranean' climate. The mediterranean climate type only occurs in five small locations within 30°-40° latitude, except for the Mediterranean Basin itself, which extends to 45° North.

The Mediterranean Sea region comprises about 60% of the world's mediterranean climate, followed by coastal areas of southern Western Australia and the Eyre Peninsula of South Australia (22%). The remaining three are much of California (between Cape Mendocino and greater Los Angeles, 10%), central Chile (5%), and the Western Cape in South Africa (3%).

True mediterranean climates are characterised by warm, dry summers with abundant sunshine and a mean daily maximum of 27°C and mild, wet winters with temperatures rarely dropping below 5°C. Whilst the Channel Islands are well outside the northern limit of the Mediterranean, our climate has some similarities that have allowed the successful establishment of many of these regions' plants.

Climate Influences

Our temperate climate is influenced by a number of important factors:

1. Any island, surrounded by water, has a much smaller annual temperature range than larger land masses at the same latitude. This is because water has a much higher heat capacity than soil and rock. Seawater takes a long time to warm up in summer, but once heated it retains its energy long after the surrounding land has cooled down, helping to moderate the climate.

2. The sea surrounding our Islands is relatively warm because it is an extension of the Gulf Stream known as the North Atlantic Drift. Although now cooler than its starting point in the Gulf of Mexico, and travelling at less than 1mph by the time it reaches us, it is sufficient to keep the coasts of the UK and north-west Europe bathed in mild humid air. The sea around our Islands rarely falls below 7°C in the winter, warming to a pleasant 18°C by August and this ensures an equable climate. By contrast, the sea in Newfoundland, at the same latitude, is 0°C in February.

3. The Islands lie within this mild westerly airflow and, although we are protected to a small extent by the English mainland in the north, and to a larger degree by the French coast that surrounds us on two other sides, we are still subjected to periods of high winds. Predominantly during the winter months, the Islands can be regularly buffeted by winds over 40mph. Whilst these winds can be a problem to gardeners, they do bring clean air straight from the Atlantic and as a result there is little pollution and light quality is high. The Islands have a good sunshine record with an average of over 1850 hours a year. (By comparison, London averages 1460 hours)

4. Driving the relatively warm current, these prevailing south-westerly winds carry a lot of moisture, and the Channel Islands have rainfall all year round. 44% of our rainfall occurs between November and February,

but, currently, we still receive 22% of our mean annual total of 810mm between May and August.

5. Together with parts of south-west Britain, our northerly latitude presents some unique problems for plants that would otherwise enjoy our temperate climate. No other place on the planet, which shares similar winter temperatures, is situated so far from the equator. Plants in the Channel Islands must endure a winter that is several months long with short days, low light levels and plenty of rain. Cold duration is much more of a problem for us than actual minimum temperature. Many exotic plants will tolerate an occasional night several degrees below zero if average temperatures are usually above 10°C, whereas weeks of temperatures below 7°C combined with high rainfall and low sunlight can test a plant's resilience to the limit. (This is the reason that the commonly quoted USDA Climate Zone system does not apply well to our situation.) Our long cool winters also mean that many exotic plants take a long time to 'get going' in the spring and, for many, their peak flowering time occurs in the early autumn. These include *Canna, Hedychium, Brugmansia* and *Dahlia*.

Local Variations

Whilst all the Channel Islands experience a very similar climate, there are variations between the islands that can have an influence on the growth of some of the more marginally hardy exotics.

The south-facing slope of Jersey allows it to receive more heat from the sun especially in the summer, when it tends to be warmer than the other Islands. By contrast, its proximity to the continent means that it is more subject to the generally colder air over France during the winter. It has an annual mean daily air temperature range of 12°C and experiences an average of nine air frosts a year. Guernsey slopes to the north, but has a more maritime influence and an annual temperature range of 10.5°C with five air frosts. Alderney, further north, more exposed to the moderating sea and windier than the other Islands, has only a 9°C difference between mean winter and summer temperatures. Sark and Herm, in the lee of Guernsey, are sheltered from some of the stronger winds and have a similar temperature to the larger Island.

In conclusion, although we are at the same latitude as northern Mongolia, or Winnipeg in Canada, we have the Gulf Stream to thank for our equable climate that allows us to grow a range of exotics from much warmer parts of the world.

Additional weather statistics appear on pages 124.-5.

Climate Change

There is now little doubt that climate change is a reality, with overwhelming evidence that human activity has caused this by significantly increasing the concentration of CO_2 in the atmosphere thereby trapping the sun's energy.

The changes that we are likely to experience are more complex than just those of 'more heat' as suggested by the term 'global warming' and the rate and amount of change are still open for discussion. What is certain is that the changes are happening rapidly.

Weather extremes

For us in the Channel Islands, we are likely to experience a rise in mean temperatures, with milder, wetter winters, hotter, drier summers, and a greater incidence of severe weather events. These changes, already apparent to the interested observer, are forecast to become commonplace within the next ten years, with weather records for 'hottest', 'driest', 'wettest' and 'windiest' being broken with increasing frequency. One study has suggested that summers as hot and dry as that of 2003 will become routine. For our gardens, this will mean that we should be able to grow a greater range of currently marginally hardy plants, but they will have to cope with weather extremes such as summer droughts and winter wet. Wind tolerance will become more important, as will salt spray tolerance, as higher winds and seas send spray further inland.

Pest pressure

The rise in mean temperatures will increase pest pressure as species previously killed off by cold winters will continue to survive outside to renew their attacks on our gardens in ever greater numbers in the spring. Pests such as red spider mite (*Tetranychus urticae*) thrive in dry summers, and vine weevil (*Otiorhynchus sulcatus*) numbers are on the increase, as the larvae are not being killed by frozen winter soils. Diseases may also be harder to combat as warmer weather will increase the threat from moulds that thrive in the new climate. There is also likely to be pest, disease and weed pressure from foreign invaders as the milder climate permits the extension of their northern boundaries. Locally, we have already seen how foreign 'warm climate' plants such as *Carpobrotus* (Hottentot Fig) can survive our winters to become invasive weeds outside the confines of the garden.

Growing season

It appears that the European growing season is getting longer, with spring coming earlier and the onset of autumn delayed well into October locally. In many places in southern Britain, it has been suggested that the growing season might shift to November through to June as plants become subjected to drought-induced 'dormancy' during the summer period. This is typical of a 'Mediterranean' type climate.

Thoughts for the Future

The famous English country garden, with its green lawns, daffodils and delphiniums may become difficult to maintain in thirty years time, and palms, citrus trees, grapes and bougainvillea could become commonplace throughout Britain. The Channel Islands are leading this trend towards more exotic planting as we are feeling the first effects of climate change.

We can take horticultural advantage of the changes to grow more exotic plants with greater confidence in their ability to survive the winter. If we alter drainage to cope with winter wet, more succulents will thrive in the long hot summers, and there will be little need to protect tender exotics over the winter.

Whilst not forgetting that climate change is raising all kinds of other serious global issues, we should explore the exotic planting possibilities it is going to allow us in our gardens in the near future.

As a result of recent mild winters it is now easier to grow marginally hardy plants such as *Geranium maderense.*

Hints to Keep Exotics Happy

Whilst all of the common plants in this book tolerate the normal Channel Island winters without additional protection, this section is intended to give some advice on winter protection when it may be needed. Despite climate change, we may still have a period of particularly cold weather when expensive garden investments may need protection. Also, some readers may be interested in pushing the boundaries of what can be grown further north and will need winter protection for some of the borderline hardy plants.

Winter help for cold spells

The primary consideration is to give any plant a spot in the garden that is closest to its natural habitat. Many of the plants in this book need full sun, well-drained soil and protection from winter wind and wet. If you get to know your garden, you can avoid planting exotics in low-lying frost pockets, or in wet or windy corners, and give them locations where they will grow well.

Soils

Many of our sandy soils have excellent drainage, which is beneficial to many exotic plants that dislike a wet winter. Helpful ideas include:
• Incorporating plenty of grit into the soil to improve drainage.
• Planting in a raised bed or on a slope also increases drainage.
• A layer of coarse gravel will help to keep moisture away from plant crowns.
• More elaborate protection from a cloche of glass or plastic will keep rain off the crown of delicate plants.
• Winter mulches (10 to 15cm deep) include wood chips, leaf mould, straw, bracken and composted garden waste.
• For climates colder than ours, plants such as gingers, cannas, and dahlias can be lifted in the autumn and stored over the winter.

Plants

Exotic plants need protecting from cold winds and frosts. Permeable windbreaks (hedges, bamboos) are useful. Other protection can include:
• Putting tender plants in the shade of overhanging trees or shrubs to give protection from radiation frosts.
• Wrapping the stem and/or growing point of a plant with fleece or hessian (never bubble wrap as it results in condensation) or buy purpose-made woven fibre bags.

Cordyline australis wrapped for a cold snap

- Leaves of flexible-leaved exotics, like cordylines and many palms, can be gathered together and secured with twine for wind and frost protection.
- Wire netting filled with straw around small shrubs, although time-consuming, can be a valuable aid to frost protection.
- Tree ferns need a straw or bracken covering to the crown that can be held in place by bending old fronds over the top.

It is important not to wrap plants too soon and to remember to remove protection as soon as serious frosts become unlikely. Locally, the first frosts usually occur in December, and any that occur after March are often light. Even in breathable wraps, plants will become damp and weeks of mild and wet weather between frost events can result in leaf rot.

Summer help for dry spells

Whilst many of our soils are sandy with excellent drainage, they are not water retentive during a long dry spell in the summer. With hot summers forecast to become more frequent, and water conservation an increasingly important issue, here are a few hints for water management.
- Plan new gardens with the climate trend in mind. Mediterranean style gardens can look as attractive as any other with the advantage of less reliance on summer rainfall.
- New plantings will benefit from the incorporation of a small diameter drainage pipe placed vertically next to the plant allowing you to pour water down to where it is needed, with no wastage.
- Water-permeable membrane can be laid over new borders. Place plants through holes and then cover the surface with decorative mulch.
- For established plants, mounding the soil in a raised ring will allow any applied water to remain within the 'moat' and reach the roots quickly before evaporating.

- Drip irrigation lines or seep hose are ideal, if more expensive, ways to irrigate in the summer as water is applied slowly, allowing it to sink into the root area.
- Hanging baskets and patio pots and planters benefit from the incorporation of water absorbent gel.
- Line unglazed terracotta pots with a plastic bag or bin liner, (making a small hole in the bottom), to reduce the evaporation of water through the sides of the pot.

Water Conservation

Irrigating the garden during the summer is likely to become an expensive use of treated drinking water and possibly socially unacceptable as well. A greater emphasis needs to be placed on other methods of water saving. Rain water is better for plants as it does not include the chlorine that treated tap water contains and should be stored wherever possible.
- Many Island homes were once on soak-away waste systems and many old tanks still exist at the bottom of the garden. These cesspits make ideal water collection chambers during the wet winter months and a small pump will allow the use of this stored water during summer droughts.
- Drainpipe diverters are easy to fit and allow the rain falling on our roofs to be collected in water butts for use in dry spells.
- Serious gardeners will also use so-called 'grey' water saved from doing the dishes, rinsing clothes, emptying the fish tank, even from showering!

If additional water is needed in a hot spell, it should be applied in the evening or early morning to prevent evaporation in the heat of the day. Do not water foliage, but apply the water to the soil near the roots. Finally, it is better to water deeply every four or five days than to give a light sprinkling every night which never penetrates very far into the soil.

Palms

There are two common palms in the Channel Islands; *Trachycarpus fortunei* and *Phoenix canariensis*, as well as *Cordyline australis* that is, in fact, not a palm at all, but is commonly thought of as one so I have included it in this section. The Cordylines, in particular, are largely responsible for the 'tropical' look that the Islands have and nothing beats a palm tree for exotic appeal!

Phoenix canariensis, St. Brelade, Jersey

Cordyline australis
New Zealand Cabbage Tree

This has to be my favourite local exotic plant, and the one that really got me interested in the foreign imports our Islands have been enjoying since the mid-1600s.

The *Cordyline* genus was originally thought to be part of the Lily family and it has been reclassified several times. What is certain, however, is that it is *not* a true palm, despite the common British name of 'Torbay' or 'Cornish' palm.

It is probably the commonest 'exotic' in the Islands with many in private and public gardens and large specimens used for waterfront landscaping projects. Originally from New Zealand, specimens were brought back to Britain in 1823 but there are also some sources that say seeds came back with Cook's third voyage that would put the date back to the late 18th century. The first ones were planted in the warmer climate of the Channel Islands in the late 19th century. The common name of cabbage tree comes from the Maori custom of cooking the apex of the plant as a vegetable.

C. australis is characterised by long leathery leaves arising from a trunk that is fast-growing under local conditions. These arching leaves are up to 90cm long and, in the common variety, a pale green. In summer, mature trees bear tiny cream flowers in large sprays with a scent that attracts large numbers of bees. They will grow up to 10m in their native habitat; here it is nearer 7m. The trunk is deeply fissured and care must be taken not to damage it as, being a monocot, it will not heal over, as would a normal tree. Cordylines produce a very long tap root that gives it great stability in a windy site, so it is best to plant young pot-raised plants in our coastal sites, rather than root-balled large specimens that will not be able to anchor themselves well for several years.

The green form is the hardiest, surviving the occasional low of −9°C when mature. All are evergreen and young specimens can be protected from cold spells by pulling up the leaves and wrapping with fleece. By the time the plant is too tall to protect in this way (after 5-7 years from a 60cm young plant) it will be capable of surviving our normal winters unprotected. Occasionally, exceptionally cold winters like that of 1963 or the more recent cold snaps of 1987 and 1991, will

Cordylines along Guernsey's coast

Cordyline australis
in flower

result in the tops of *Cordylines* being frosted and dying back. Usually the plant will re-shoot from below the damaged part, or more often, from the base of the trunk.

Once Cordylines are mature, usually around 5-7 years, they will flower in late spring. Sometimes a plant may flower when younger, usually as a response to drought stress while being grown in a pot. After flowering, the trunk will fork into two heads, which will each flower and divide the following year, building up a large multi-headed crown after a number of years. The flower sprays are best removed after flowering to avoid seedlings coming up like grass for several years around the base of the plants. Variegated forms rarely flower and do not divide, growing only as a single-trunked specimen.

Green forms of *C. australis* are the hardiest, whilst some of the purple forms are very susceptible to rotting in our cool wet winters. Pot specimens of these are best allowed to become almost dry before protecting from further rain in an unheated green-house or conservatory whilst those grown outside must be on very free draining soil.

There are numerous varieties of *Cordyline australis* and various other hybrids between other cordyline species. The ones below are those that I have found to be reliably hardy outside in recent winters.

C. australis All the green types are the most common and hardiest of all.

'**Sundance**' is fast growing, with a central red stripe to the green leaves.

'**Red Star**' has a good deep red colour, and prefers drier conditions than the green types.

'**Red Sensation**' has long purple leaves with a central red vein; it is fast growing and very attractive.

'**Coffee Cream**' is a brown leafed version with a cream stripe, not to everyone's taste.

'**Variegata**', '**Dazzler**' and '**Sparkler**' are all cream/pink/green striped leaf versions and all beautiful.

'**Pacific Series**' is a relatively new collection to come out of New Zealand with stripes in various shades of pink and coral. The hardiness is not fully established but they are attractive plants if you want something flamboyant.

Phoenix canariensis
Canary Island Date Palm

Mature *Phoenix canariensis*,
Candie Gardens, Guernsey

This genus of mostly single-stemmed palms with feather-shaped leaves contains about 17 species but only one is known to grow with ease locally. All *Phoenix* palms have feather leaves consisting of a single rib, with many 'valley-shaped' leaflets extending from it in a single plane. Often the lowest of these are reduced to short (sharp!) spines.

P. canariensis (AGM) originates from the Canary Islands where they grow to 15m with a stout trunk marked with diamond leaf scars from old fronds. This is the hardiest species and is becoming more widely planted in the Islands. In our climate they are relatively slow growing and can be kept in a large pot for many years, growing to 1m after 5 years from seed. If you do want to plant it in the ground, ensure that you leave sufficient space around it to develop as the leaves can be up to 6m long, and the trunk may eventually reach 1m in diameter.

P. canariensis likes fertile, moist but well-drained soil and grows best in a lightly shaded position although it seems to tolerate full sunshine in our northern climate. Regular feeding encourages faster growth. They are very easy to raise from seed, although germination can take some months. The plants are generally pest and disease free.

The older the plant, the hardier it will be and temperatures down to −5°C should be no problem to a plant over 5 years old, provided it is not in cold water-logged soil. All plants will survive the cold better if kept dry, and a fleece wrap over the leaves is beneficial when a radiation frost is forecast. Mature plants in sheltered locations locally have survived −10°C, but these have been on very well-drained soil.

Jersey and Guernsey have some fine examples of *P. canariensis*. The easiest to view are the ones along the seafronts at Gorey in Jersey and St. Peter Port in Guernsey. There is a very old specimen in Candie Gardens in Guernsey.

Trachycarpus fortunei

Chusan Palm

A common sight around the Islands, *Trachycarpus fortunei* (AGM) probably originated from China and is one of the hardiest palms known. Often thought to be tender, they are popular locally but can be grown throughout the UK where they will survive short spells to −18°C when mature. They are slow growing, supposedly reaching 15m after 50 years; my grandfather planted two in Jersey in the 1930s and they are 'only' 9m tall. The windy conditions here must limit their stature to an extent.

All *Trachycarpus* species are single-stemmed evergreen palms with a head of stiff fan-shaped leaves, each up to 75cm long. When mature, they bear small yellow flowers in large clusters every summer that develop into dark blue fruit on female plants. *T. fortunei* is distinguishable from other fan palms by the dense brown fibrous hairs that cover the trunk, but these can be removed to leave a smooth surface if preferred. Older brown or shredded leaves can be cut off to maintain a tidy appearance to the plant.

Although it is recommended growing this palm in sheltered locations to avoid the wind shredding the fan leaves, it will tolerate a windy site but the leaves will probably develop brown tips and look rather untidy.

It will grow in full sun, but leaf colour and size are best in a shady location.

There are some specimens growing in a disused quarry along the railway walk near St. Aubin in Jersey that hardly ever see any direct sunlight but are growing well, with each fan measuring some 100cm across.

Trachycarpus can be grown in a large pot on the patio, but will grow slightly more quickly if put in the soil and given a good feed each spring and regular water in dry spells. This palm doesn't mind a heavy soil as long as it does not get waterlogged but it does not like drought or excessive heat. Whilst small and 'mobile', it can be sheltered

Trachycarpus fortunei in flower in May

from the worst of the winter weather in a cold glasshouse but as long as it is not so cold as to freeze the soil it will cope out of the wind outside. A wrapping of fleece will protect the leaves of small specimens in the ground. By the time *Trachycarpus* is too large to wrap it will be hardy enough to cope with the worst of the cold and snow that we can get in some winters.

There are many examples of *T. fortunei* throughout the Islands with some tall specimens in Candie Gardens, Guernsey.

Mature *Trachycarpus fortunei*, Candie Gardens, Guernsey

Other Palms

There are several other palms that grow well in the Channel Islands, and gardeners are becoming more adventurous as winters have become milder, and the plants more readily available. *Chamaerops humilis*, the Mediterranean fan palm, is my personal favourite. Others that are hardy locally include *Butia* and *Jubea* from South America and *Washingtonia* from Mexico.

Butia capitata

Jelly palm

This is a hardy feather palm from the cool dry regions of South America. It can grow to 7m with long, curved, blue-green leaves. It needs full sun and plenty of water and is easy to lift and move if it starts getting too big.

There are several small examples in the Islands. It hybridizes well with *Jubea* and *Syagrus* to form other hardy specimens. It is hardy down to –8°C if kept dry.

Young
Butia capitata

Chamaerops humilis
Mediterranean Fan Palm

C. humilis has the distinction of being the only native mainland European fan palm. It has broad green leaves up to 1m long with fans of 12-15 linear leaflets radiating from the centre. When young it can be confused with *Trachycarpus*, but *Chamaerops* has sharp spines along the sides of each leaf stalk. It is slow growing, reaching 1m in height and breadth in 5 years from a typical 40cm garden centre plant. It will eventually grow to 3-4m under local conditions, producing many offsets around the base.

Originally thought to be frost tender, it is now classed as frost hardy, coping with temperatures down to –12°C as the plant matures. It should be protected from cold drying winds to prevent tip burn on the leaves, but unless very small, frost protection here is not necessary.

It grows in any free-draining soil and, once established, will produce up to 10 new fronds each year. It will grow in bright sunshine, or light shade, and although tolerating dry conditions, will grow much faster if given plenty of water during the summer and a good feed in the spring. I recommend removing the majority of the suckers from the base as they develop, to leave 3 or 5 trunks exposed. If this is not done it will grow into a thick mass of fronds with no real architectural merit, as pictured here.

This is my favourite palm for local conditions, ideal for the smaller garden, and it should be grown more widely.

Mature *Chamaerops humilis*, Sausmarez Manor, Guernsey

Jubaea chiliensis

Chilean Wine Palm

This feather palm is very slow growing, and thus expensive to buy. It is one of the hardier feather palms, coping with temperatures to −10°C if on a well-drained site. It differs from other common feather palms in having 'roof-shaped' leaflets, as opposed to 'valley-shaped'. Eventually it grows a vast trunk up to 2m in diameter and will grow for hundreds of years if happy…one for the grandchildren to enjoy!

Jubea chiliensis

Washingtonia filifera

Californian Cotton Palm

Easy to find in garden centres, this fast growing palm has large fan leaves with many thread-like filaments along the leaf edges. Established plants show good cold resistance down to –10°C. It can grow to 20m. There are many young plants in gardens around the Islands and a 5m specimen at the entrance to St Peter's Garden Centre, Jersey.

A closely related species is *Washingtonia robusta* (the Skyduster or Mexican Fan Palm) that can grow to an alarming 25m or more. It is very similar in appearance to *W. filifera* when young, but has a slimmer trunk as it matures. Its cold tolerance is not established but may do well in a sheltered sunny site. The amusingly named hybrid of the two, *W. filibusta*, combines the rapid growth of *W. robusta* with the hardiness of *W. filifera*. All are easy to raise from seed.

Washingtonia filifera fronds

Spiky Plants

All of these plants are found throughout the Islands, originally imported from more exotic parts of the world. Agave and Yucca are from desert areas of the Americas, *Phormium* from New Zealand and *Echium* from southern Europe. Most spiky plants evolved spines as a defence against being eaten by hungry animals. They are most suited to dry soils and do well in full sun.

Yucca gloriosa '**Variegata**'

Agave americana

Century Plant

Whilst not, perhaps, the first plant that springs to mind when you think of our exotic plants, the agave is ideally suited to our light soils and mild climate, and is hardier than it is given credit for.

This genus of rosette-forming succulents has over two hundred species, most of which originated in the desert and mountain regions of North and South America. They are characterised by a vicious spike that tops the rigid, fleshy leaves, and many have toothed margins also.

Agaves were called Century Plants as they were thought to take a hundred years to flower. This is not the case, with plants flowering after 20 or so years, usually after a long hot summer the previous year. The flower spikes are up to 8m tall, with greenish-yellow flowers that last for several weeks and act as a magnet for bees for miles around. Unfortunately the rosette dies after flowering, although it has usually produced many offsets by this time.

All agaves thrive on very free draining soil, so unless you are blessed with sandy soil, add a lot of grit to the soil before you plant one of these outside, and plant it on a south facing, sunny site, ensuring that the spines will be well out of the way of passers-by. Raised beds and slopes also work well to ensure good drainage.

The most common species in the islands is *A. americana* (AGM) that is relatively slow growing in pots, but will reach a mature size of 2m x 3m inside 10 years in suitable soil. It is often listed as half-hardy (surviving down to 0°C) but there are several specimens on the Islands that survived the last really cold

Agave americana in bloom, Gorey, Jersey

winter in 1991 (with a ground frost of –15°C, air –8°C). Whilst the green form is striking, more attractive are the variegated forms '**Marginata**' with cream edges, and '**Mediopicta**' with a cream central band to each leaf. '**Mediopicta Alba**' has a white central band. These will tolerate –5°C.

Agave americana, St. Brelade, Jersey

There is a lovely example of *A. americana* '**Marginata**' on the sea wall in La Collette Gardens, and a superb grey/green *A. americana* opposite Woodbine Corner, St. Brelade, both in Jersey. Guernsey has several variegated plants in Candie Gardens.

Agave americana '**Mediopicta Alba**'

Echium pininana

Tower of Jewels

Probably brought here by the large Madeiran population as a reminder of home, although originally from the Canaries, this plant is now common in Island gardens and may be seen soon in the wild as it seeds itself freely.

Echium is a genus of some 40 species of rosette-forming stiffly hairy annuals, biennials and perennials from Southern Europe and Africa. They have funnel-shaped flowers, each only 1-2cm long, massed on spikes that grow up to 4 metres high in some species.

E. pininana, the Giant Echium, is the species seen commonly in the Islands. In its first year it produces a rosette of hairy, lance-shaped leaves. In its second or third year each rosette produces a long, loosely flowered, spike between 1 and 4 metres tall that grows rapidly from early spring, flowering in early summer. The flowers are blue with large green bracts. Occasionally, the spikes can begin growing in the autumn, to flower in May the following year. The flowering rosette will then die. The plant will self-seed very easily to provide plants each year if left to its own devices.

They are well able to withstand exposure to our coastal breezes and salt-laden winds but the flower spike may be worth staking if your garden is very exposed. They appreciate summer moisture but show good drought tolerance and will bounce back after wilting. They have long thin tap roots that dislike transplanting, so move seedlings to their permanent position when they are small.

Occasionally the young plants will get whitefly, but are generally trouble free. The very hairy leaves may cause skin irritation

Echium pininana,
Sausmarez Manor, Guernsey

however, so be careful when handling the plants.

E. candicans (syn. *E. fastuosum)* is called the 'Pride of Madeira', but this variety is less common than its more showy relative. This is an open woody shrub with leaves in a rosette and many dense spikes, about 30cm long, of purple-blue flowers that are produced in the summer. There are pale blue and white forms also. It reaches a height of 1.5m with a 1.2m spread. *E. wildpretii* has deep pink spikes. All of the above are frost tender species, unhappy below +2°C, although they will cope with temperatures down to −3°C in a sheltered spot. To help with winter protection, cover first year plants with fleece or hessian if cold weather threatens and keep on the dry side if possible.

There are *Echiums* of both species in many public gardens throughout the Islands.

Echium candicans,
Coronation Park, Jersey

Echium wildpretii, Herm

Phormium

New Zealand Flax

The flowing form of *Phormium cookianum*

This is another plant from New Zealand that is ideally suited to the mild coastal conditions of the Channel Islands. The Maori used the leaves for weaving baskets, mats, and the fibres were used for making clothing, fishing nets, and ropes, hence the common name of flax.

These evergreen perennials have sword-like leaves, without the fearsome spikes of Agaves, and make wonderful architectural additions to any garden. The other big advantage is that they are actually quite hardy, and will survive short periods down to –10°C.

Phormiums are very salt-tolerant and grow well in exposed coastal sites, in a wide variety of soil types. Although they do not grow well in very dry soils, they will tolerate them and they are quite adaptable to shade or sun. Phormiums are clump forming, but fairly slow growing, taking several years to reach their maximum size of 2-3m across. They look especially good planted in gravel gardens, alongside grasses. They are susceptible to mealy bug infestation, especially in dry, sheltered sites, but are generally disease free.

There are two species and over 80 cultivars. *P. tenax* forms large clumps of stiff leathery leaves up to 3 metres high. There is a pronounced central fold to the leaves and the plants are usually sombre in colour. This is the hardier of the two species. *P. cookianum* has softer, more floppy, leaves and is available in a wide variety of coloured forms. It reaches a maximum of 2m in height. There are also a number of vivid hybrids available. My favourites are **'Yellow Wave'** (AGM) in shades of green and yellow, and **'Jester'** a bright pink with green leaf margins.

Colourful stripes of *Phormium* **'Jester'**

Both species produce tall spikes with groups of tubular orange or yellow flowers in the summer; these spikes tower to 4m in some cases. They are unusual rather than attractive and can be cut down once flowering is over or they will persist on the plant for several months.

Sometimes the coloured versions can revert to green, or muddy brown forms as they age and if this is not to your liking, they are best replaced, although the newer forms seem a lot more stable. An occasional section may revert by itself and this can be carefully removed to leave the remainder.

There are examples all over the Islands with plenty in public gardens such as Howard Davis Park in Jersey and Candie Gardens in Guernsey.

Phormium tenax in bloom

Yucca

This is the plant to grow for a truly exotic effect in your garden. All varieties have large sword like leaves and tall spikes with bell-like white flowers. Despite their tropical origin (Central America) and liking for hot, dry conditions several of the thirty-plus species are surprisingly hardy in Britain.

The beauty of many yuccas is that once they are established (2-3 years after planting out a small plant) they will flower reliably every summer, doing particularly well in hot years. All prefer good drainage and full sun to encourage annual flowering. The rosette of leaves remains compact on the stem-less varieties and will reach a maximum of 90cm high.

Y. filamentosa (AGM) (Adam's Needle) has a basal rosette of 60cm long stiff leaves with loose white threads along the edges. It is, perhaps, the most commonly planted species locally. **'Bright Edge'** (AGM) has a yellow edge to the leaves and the leaves of **'Variegata'** (AGM) are striped with cream. They both produce a 2m tall flower stalk with creamy-white bells up to 5cm long in the summer. They will eventually form clumps, spreading by underground rhizomes. All *Y. filamentosa* are fully hardy (to –20°C) and are often used locally in public planting schemes. There are some nice examples of these on the roundabout coming into town from Elizabeth Harbour, Jersey.

As its name suggests, *Y. gloriosa* (AGM) (Spanish Dagger) has a nasty spike at each leaf tip so is best planted away from paths. It is hardy to –8°C, and well below this if kept dry. Locally it grows to a maximum of 2m on a short trunk, with dark green, lightly pleated leaves. The flower spike can reach a further 2.5m with large white bell-like flowers. This species is often confused with (and mislabelled as) *Y. recurvifolia*, which has more strongly curved leaves.

Y. elephantipes (AGM) (Giant or Spineless Yucca) is slightly different in that it will grow into a small tree. It is usually sold as a houseplant with a stout trunk and two or more rosettes of bright green leaves sprouting from the top. It is supposed

Yucca gloriosa **'Variegata'** in flower

to grow at temperatures above 10°C only, but constraints of space have resulted in many being planted outside when they outgrow the house! Mine has now survived two winters outside (min. –3°C) with no protection, and is over 2.5m tall. They will probably tolerate –7°C for short spells. The slightly soft leaves are susceptible to hail damage however, and benefit from a wrapping of fleece in cold spells. In their native Mexico, they can grow to 10m and produce spikes of cream flowers in late summer but they rarely flower locally. They produce side shoots that can be left on for a bushy plant or removed and potted up for a year before being planted elsewhere in the garden. Like all the Yuccas, it is very drought tolerant, but appreciates a good high nitrogen feed in the spring and an occasional summer watering.

Above: *Yucca filamentosa* blooms amongst a sea of *Agapanthus*

Left: The exotic form of *Yucca elephantipes* does well outside

Other Spiky Plants

Many enthusiastic local gardeners, as well as public gardens, have recently planted some of the more unusual spiky plants, and although some of them are only marginally hardy, many do well on light sandy soils, especially if kept dry in the winter.

Astelia chathamica & A. nervosa

These evergreen perennials from New Zealand have arching silvery leaves up to 1.5m long and grow to become clumps some 2m wide. The former is the larger, reaching 1.2m in height, the latter half this.

Both grow well in full sun, but like a moist soil, and do not mind some light shade if this is necessary to maintain moist soil. They are hardy to –5°C, perhaps lower for *A. nervosa*, as long as they are not waterlogged in the winter. '**Silver Spear**' is a commonly found silver leaf form, and '**Westland**' a bronze. They also make good pot specimens.

Astelia '**Silver Spear**'

Beschorneria yuccoides
Mexican Lily

Beschorneria yuccoides in June, Rozel, Jersey

There are many examples of this yucca look-alike around the Islands. It is a striking plant with narrow blue-green leaves in a rosette up to 1.5m wide. In the spring it produces a large arching spike over 2m tall, which is rosy red with nodding yellow-green flowers. The rosette then dies but by this stage the plant has normally produced numerous other rosettes to continue the display for following years. They are hardy to –6°C if grown dry and are best suited to a slope, where the arching flower stems can be seen at their best. Slugs and snails love the leaves on this one.

Fascicularia

This is from the Bromeliad family and will survive in almost pure gravel, and it does well in some of the more sandy local soils. It originates from Central Chile and is frost hardy to –5°C when grown dry. There are two species, *F. bicolor* and *F. pitcairniifolia*, both with low growing rosettes of spiky green leaves and central blue flowers in the summer. The bases of the leaves nearest the centre turn bright red at flowering and it is best planted on a slope, so that the coloured centre is easily seen. *F. pitcairniifolia* has arguably the better red colouration and is the larger plant, slowly growing up to 1m wide.

Fascicularia bicolor

Furcraea

Also from Central America, the *Furcraea* is much less common locally but, like the *Beschorneria*, it produces such a fabulous flower spike that it really ought to be planted more often. The leaves grow from a central rosette, rather like a yucca, and are quite stiff and olive-green or variegated depending on the variety. They need a large garden as they can grow over 2m tall and wide. After a few years, a large spike is produced in the summer, growing slowly over the following year to produce numerous bell-shaped flowers the next summer. In some species many small plantlets develop along the stems and these can be picked off and planted up elsewhere. The flower stem will last for the rest of the year while the leaves die off. There are usually several other rosettes around the base to continue the display in future years. They are only hardy to –3°C and are best grown in dry soil near the coast.

There are several plants of *F. longaeva* on the approach to Elizabeth Harbour, Jersey.

Furcraea longaeva in bloom, Herm

Puya

From the same family and origin as the *Fascicularia*, the *Puya* is a locally rare but stunning plant in flower. The name 'Puya' was derived from the Mapuche Indian word meaning 'point' and a close look at the long thin leaves of this plant shows why. The silvery foliage has curved, hooked spines along the edges that can trap an unwary hand or even a small animal. All varieties form a slow growing clump and enjoy very dry, well-drained soil. Most are hardy to –6°C in these conditions.

The variety seen locally is *P. alpestris* with a 1m wide rosette producing a 1.5m tall spike of turquoise-blue flowers with orange stamens in the summer, when about five years old. The bare tips to the flowering branches are used as perches for birds seeking nectar in their native Chile. *P. chiliensis* is similar, with lime-green flowers on an equally impressive spike. *P. mirabilis* produces an elegant spike with delicate lime-coloured blooms in September.

All *Puya* are monocarpic (the rosette dies after flowering), but most are clump forming and there will be many offsets that will continue to grow and flower in subsequent years.

Top right: Unusual turquoise flowers on *Puya alpestris*

Below right: A spiky clump of *Puya chiliensis*

Succulents

Preferring dry conditions, all the succulents on the Islands need soils with very sharp drainage, and do well in the poor soils on many of the coastal cliffs. *Carpobrotus*, in particular, has naturalised widely and *Lampranthus* could well do the same if we continue to have the mild winters of recent years.

Lampranthus spectabilis

Carpobrotus edulis

Hottentot Fig

Local opinion on this plant is very much divided. Originally from South Africa and closely related to *Lampranthus,* it has escaped from gardens and is now threatening the indigenous flora around our coasts where it flourishes in the sparse soil along the cliffs.

Like the Ice Plant, *Carpobrotus edulis* has fleshy stems and 3-angled leaves that are green but often tinged red in extreme drought. It is a prostrate ground cover plant that is widely used in California for stabilizing new soil banks along their highways. Known here as the Hottentot Fig, it produces edible, fig-like, brown fruit in the autumn, but these are yet to become a local delicacy!

Pink-flowered *Carpobrotus edulis*

The plant is described as growing to 15cm tall with, ominously, indefinite spread. Whilst it produces large (8-12cm) pink or yellow flowers rather sparsely in the summer, the very fact that it is so prolific means that many smaller, local, wild plants are swamped. Old growth forms a dense brown mat that prevents all other plant growth and only thorough removal by hand, or a severe frost, will kill it. Its weight can also destabilise crumbling cliffs. Our recent winters have been mild and although efforts have been made to remove it from some of the more sensitive areas, it remains widespread. It does have some beneficial aspects, in that it is quite fire-resistant, unlike Gorse (*Ulex* spp.) and it can prevent erosion.

The RHS list *C. edulis* as a half-hardy plant with a minimum requirement of 7°C but it certainly survives down to –3°C locally, with the roots probably coping with even lower. It is only suitable as a garden plant in sun-baked, dry areas and does very poorly in a pot where it never flowers.

Common in all the Islands, there are some large areas growing near the cliff path between St Brelade's Bay and Corbière in Jersey, and on the west coast of Guernsey.

Lampranthus spectabilis

Ice Plant

Related to the Hottentot Fig and another native of South Africa, this is a fast growing ground cover plant with glorious daisy-like flowers in shades of pink and magenta. It is a succulent that adores hot, sunny, sharply drained soil and is commonly seen cascading down sloping banks, over walls and in rockeries. The leaves are pale green, 3-angled and succulent, often reddening in full sun.

It is well suited to coastal conditions and poor, dry soils, but will benefit from an occasional feed and water in a long hot summer, but do not overdo either or it will not flower well. This is the perfect ground cover plant for a sun-baked seaside garden. The one draw back of *Lampranthus* is the very short flowering season in June. Dead-heading is time consuming and fiddly, but will encourage a later bloom of flowers, although this is rarely as good as the first and often hardly worth the effort. They can become woody with age and don't like pruning so are best replaced if this occurs.

There are various other species of *Lampranthus*, and hybrids in various shades of pink and apricot, but all perform pretty much the same. *Lampranthus* are closely related to other succulents, known collectively as Mesembryanthemums and the Livingstone Daisy (*Dorotheanthus criniflorus*), many of which are not hardy.

There are no real problems with pests and diseases, although slugs will occasionally nibble the flower stalks and I have seen sparrows pecking at the flowers, possibly in

Lampranthus spectabilis, St. Ouen, Jersey

a hunt for nectar.

If acclimatised to cool winters and kept dry, it will cope with the occasional night of –3°C. In marginally hardy areas, a covering of fleece on frosty nights gives an extra degree of protection, but do not leave the plants covered longer than necessary otherwise rot may develop.

There is a superb collection of *L. spectabilis* on the cliffs above L'Etacq, St Ouen in Jersey, planted by Mr Blampied. The best time to see them is on a sunny day in June when the tapestry of light and dark pinks is visible from La Corbière, over three miles away.

Other Succulents

Local gardeners who have very sandy soil, and perhaps despair of finding plants to grow well, can use any of these succulents that will thrive in such conditions. They work especially well in gravel gardens where they can remain relatively dry over the winter. Excellent drainage is the key to success with any of these succulent plants.

Aeonium arboreum

The Aeonium is a succulent perennial that really is growing at the very limit of its climatic boundaries here in the Islands, far from its natural home in the southern Mediterranean. It has soft fleshy leaves that grow in a rosette, and eventually grows a trunk and branches like a miniature tree.

Most species are found in the Canary Islands off the west coast of Africa, but *A. arboreum* (AGM) comes from Morocco. The green-leaved form of the species, commonest in the wild, has been grown in Europe since 1727. It can reach 1m tall. There is a lovely form with maroon leaves; *A. arboreum f. atropurpureum* and *A. arboreum* '**Schwartzkopf**' (AGM) is an extremely dark clone of this form.

All need well-drained soil, and raised beds will further aid good drainage with full sun essential in our climate. Coming from a Mediterranean climate, *Aeoniums* grow in the winter months and are dormant during the heat of summer.

In all species, individual rosettes die after blooming but the branching *A. arboreum* will continue to grow after flowering. The flowers are small, yellow and very long lasting. It will be quite happy in a pot for many years.

It can be planted outside – a south facing spot, under the rain shelter of the house eaves, is the best position. It will certainly need protection when the temperature falls below +1°C and a cutting or two kept indoors will be extra insurance.

Aeonium arboreum in flower

Aloe striatula

The Cape Province of South Africa provides us with another range of splendid plants that we can grow in our climate, the Aloes. These evergreen perennials are only hardy locally when grown on very well-drained soils in full sun but are ideal for modern gravel gardens, as they require very little maintenance. Aloes produce wonderfully exotic flower spikes of bell-shaped flowers in reds and yellows from spring to autumn.

Aloe striatula has a rosette of large, thick, fleshy leaves which grow over time to form stems. The leaves are lance-shaped with a sharp tip and short spines on the edge. The flowers are superficially like yellow red hot pokers (*Kniphofia*). It is hardy to –5°C in dry soils. It is very prone to grazing by slugs and snails. *Aloe arborescens* is a similar plant, with red flowers (to –3°C).

Aloe striatula (with slug damage!)

Echeveria secunda

Echevaria in a coastal gravel garden, Guernsey

Sometimes confused with *Sempervivum*, the similar looking *Echeveria* are not particularly hardy, whereas *Sempervivum* are completely hardy. Only two of the 150 species of *Echeveria*, from Mexico and Central America, are slightly hardy, tolerating a minimum of –3°C in sheltered locations. They are *E. secunda glauca* (AGM) and *E. secunda*. Both are clump forming, with rosettes of wedge-shaped succulent grey leaves that bear short spikes of red flowers in the summer.

Sempervivum

I have included this as an excellent alternative for the 'desert' look garden if you are worried about the hardiness of *Echeveria*. *Sempervivum* is completely hardy if grown with good drainage. The Latin name actually means 'always alive' and they will take at least −15°C with no problem. There are hundreds of species that come in a range of colours and sizes, and all are clump-forming rosettes that spread by producing new 'babies' each year. When a rosette produces the tall spike of tiny flowers, it will die afterwards but by this stage there are many new rosettes to take over. They make good ground cover and also do well in shallow pots where their spread can be limited.

Sempervivum growing in a granite wall

View of St. Aubin's Bay, Jersey, with *Cordyline australis* and Thrift *(Armeria)*

Daisies

Many of the more exotic daisies in the Islands came from the Mediterranean, whilst others arrived here, brought by plant hunters from travels to South Africa. All have in common their liking for full sun and very well drained soil to flower at their best.

Hardy white *Osteospermum*

Argyranthemum

Marguerite Daisy

Argyranthemum are from the Canary Islands and Madeira where they grow from the coasts right up to volcanic mountains at 2,300m high. Whilst the highest point in any of the Channel Islands is only around 140m the weather in our Islands is considerably cooler in the winter and many *Argyranthemum* will not survive below –2°C unless in very well-drained soil and out of drying winds. However, they do work hard in local gardens, flowering continuously from spring right through into early winter.

The leaves are finely dissected green to grey-green, and the daisy-like flowers can be single, double or anemone-like, and, unlike the similar looking *Euryops*, they can be white, apricot, red or pale pink, as well as lemon yellow.

Young plants are best kept in pots to overwinter, and a deep, dry mulch can be used to protect plants in the ground, with some fleece covering when frost is expected. Sometimes the plants will re-grow from the base if the top is frosted, but it may be worth taking cuttings as insurance against loss of prized specimens.

Popular varieties include *A.* '**Cornish Gold**' (AGM) and *A.* '**Jamaica Primrose**' (AGM) both of which have yellow flowers. *A. frutescens* and *A. foeniculaceum* have large white daisy flowers while *A.* '**Vancouver**' has double pink flowers.

Argyranthemum foeniculaceum, Candie Gardens, Guernsey

Erigeron

Erigeron glaucus

 A large genus with over two hundred species of annuals, biennials and perennials, this has two species that are often found growing wild around the Islands although they were originally introduced as garden plants. Both are fully hardy (to −15°C) although their origins may lead one into thinking that they prefer a hot and arid climate.

E. *glaucus* is known as the Beach Aster in its native California and it is commonly found along sandy coastlines along with sea lavender (*Limonium latifolium*). It is a low growing spreading perennial with soft grey-green leaves that produces large (4-6cm across) daisy-like flowers in late spring. The petals are usually pale lilac but there are pink forms and both have wide yellow centres. It is ideally suited to hot dry areas of the garden, or creeping over paving stones, and does well in our coastal gardens.

E. *karvinskianus* (AGM) (syn. E. *mucronatus)* comes from Mexico and is another carpeting perennial but with loose, branching stems and finely divided leaves. In the summer it produces numerous white daisy-sized flowers that fade to pink. It has escaped from gardens and is now seen in many of our granite walls where the very dry conditions suit it. It was first recorded in the British Isles growing in Guernsey where it is known as the St. Peter Port Daisy. In the USA it is known as the Santa Barbara Daisy (or Fleabane) and is recommended for areas where water conservation is important, as well as for attracting beneficial insects to the garden, jobs it does well locally too.

Erigiron karvinskianus in a
Jersey granite wall

Euryops

Golden Daisy Bush

Another wonderful introduction from southern Africa, the Golden Daisy Bush thrives in our climate and is usually covered with bright yellow daisy-like flowers all year round. This is a particularly cheering sight in the cold rain of February and it is seen in many public gardens.

This is an easy to grow plant, quickly producing a bush some 1.2m high and 2m across. It has finely divided grey-green leaves with bright yellow flowers 5cm across, borne on long stalks. These are either single or in groups of two or three.

E. pectinatus (AGM) is common in the Islands and it is borderline hardy, surviving temperatures to –3°C or so if out of chilling winds that can desiccate the foliage. *Euryops* will take a good pruning if it gets too big, but when it is almost always in flower, there never seems to be a 'good time'. I think you need to grit your teeth and give it a good haircut in late spring. Also seen locally is *E. chrysanthemoides* with green leaves. *Euryops* are often confused with the more tender *Argyranthemum*, as both are widely grown on the islands.

Nice plants of *E. pectinatus* can be seen at the eastern entrance to the road tunnel beneath Fort Regent in Jersey. These generally bloom all winter, and are making an attractive low growing hedge along the path.

Euryops chrysanthemoides

Osteospermum

African Daisy

This popular plant is generally known as a summer bedding plant but it is a perennial with some varieties quite capable of surviving from year to year in the Islands.

Osteospermum have long green leaves, often with lobed edges, and grow to 60cm tall, with indefinite spread for some of the more prostrate varieties – if they are happy, the stems will root into the soil as they grow. Large (5-8cm) daisy-like flowers are borne from late spring into the autumn. These are commonly white or pink, but there has been a wealth of breeding in recent years and there are now a whole range of colours and habits available.

Their native mountainous habitat in southern Africa is a good indicator of the conditions they enjoy most. To grow flourishing *Osteospermum*, it is vital that they are given a very free-draining situation; they have little tolerance for continuously damp or saturated soil.

Hot summer weather, combined with drought, can sometimes halt flower production, but cutting back the plants and deadheading usually ensures good regrowth and more flowers in the autumn when temperatures cool. Occasionally these hot dry conditions will encourage mildew growth on the leaves. Daily misting, or the use of a fungicide should stop this problem. All *Osteospermum* close their flowers in the afternoon, but newer hybrids are now showing longer opening, and greater tolerance of shade.

Varieties of *O. jucundum*, especially **'Blackthorn Seedling'**, are the most hardy and tend to have purple, pink or white flowers. These will survive –5°C. Some of the most unusual and attractive *Osteospermum* have spoon-shaped petals, or variegated foliage, but they are not fully hardy and are likely to die when the temperature dips below 0°C.

Many of the new hybrids are bred especially for pot growth and these can be brought under shelter and kept barely moist over the winter if you live in an area susceptible to frost.

Osteospermum in peach and lemon shades

Other Daisies

Many of our local daisies come from southern Africa, and are usually treated as annual summer bedding plants, although several will survive a mild winter to flower again the following year.

Arctotis

Sometimes known as *Venidium*, these large South African daisies grow well in our Mediterranean-like summers, but can suffer in the long wet winters and are often treated as annuals. They have silver leaves and solitary, brightly coloured flower heads on long (40cm) stems, borne from midsummer onwards. They are worth growing in a pot, plunging this in the border for the summer. Colours available include white, yellow, orange, pink and red. The closely related *Arctotheca* is hardier (to –5°C) but only comes with yellow flowers.

Arctotis

Brachyscome iberidifolia and B. multifida

Brachyscome's delicate blue flowers

From Australia, the Swan River Daisies are hanging basket and rockery stars with feathery green foliage. Commonly blue-flowered, there are pink and lilac varieties too. As long as they are sheltered from temperatures below –1°C they can live for several years. They have similar flowers to *Felicia amelloides* that will tolerate –3°C.

Gazania

A bright orange *Gazania* hybrid

 From African meadows, most Gazania will survive the occasional night at –1°C but are quite tender and can be given a layer of fleece for extra protection. They must be kept on the dry side for the winter.

Sanvitalia procumbens

 This is a stunning hardy little plant from California and Mexico. It produces tiny daisy-like flowers in bright yellow or orange throughout the summer with no deadheading needed. It flowers right into December, then dies down to come up again in the spring. It is a real performer.

Sanvitalia flowers into the autumn

Pink shades of *Osteospermum*

Climbers

Climbers add height to a garden or border, and can be either trained over a pergola, or allowed to self-cling up a wall. The following three varieties are common in the Islands and are hardier than many people realise.

Passiflora caerulea in bloom in July

Campsis radicans

Trumpet Vine

This vigorous woody climber is originally from south-eastern North America. It has lovely dark green pinnate leaves and wonderful clusters of 4-12 dark orange trumpets in late summer. Although a climber to 10 metres, it is not self-clinging for several years and will need sturdy support until it establishes itself. It is fully frost-hardy, coping with temperatures down to –15°C, but grows best against a south-facing wall. This allows it to accumulate enough heat to ripen the wood and encourage development of the flowers.

The attractive leaves, with seven or more leaflets, are deciduous, and the dark orange blooms, each up to 7cm long, are borne on the current season's growth. Pruning can be carried out in late spring, cutting back to 3 buds, and they will eventually have a 5 x 4m spread. They must not dry out in summer, but do not mind thin sandy soils where they produce the best flowers. *Campsis* have a reputation for being reluctant to flower but this is usually only the case if they are being grown in too rich a soil, or in the shade. After being allowed to establish properly, they will flower in profusion in a sunny site.

C. radicans is available in several colours; **'Indian Summer'** is one of the best orange types; **'Yellow Trumpet'** and **'Flava'** (AGM) have yellow flowers. *C.* x *taglibuana* **'Madam Galen'** (AGM) is widely available and has deep orange flowers with a red throat.

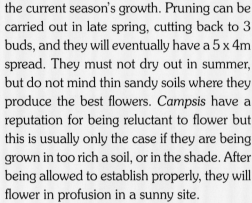

Several private gardens have large examples; the lovely *Campsis* along the road opposite Grouville Church in Jersey pops over the granite wall to impress passers-by with its flamboyant flowers. There are also several examples in nearby St. Malo and St. Servan, France.

Campsis radicans **'Flamenco'**

Jasminum officinale

Jasmine

There are two basic groups of jasmine, many of which originate in China. The bushy types with yellow flowers are hardy, and the climbing jasmines that twine, usually with white or pink flowers, are all rather tender. They are sometimes confused with *Trachelospernum jasminoides*, another slightly tender climber.

Of the climbers, *J. officinale* (AGM) is the most common in the Channel Islands. It is woody with pinnate dark green leaves comprising 5-9 pointed leaflets. It produces clusters of fragrant star-like white flowers, some 2cm across, in the summer. Here in the Islands it is often ever-green, but can be deciduous if temperatures drop below –4°C. It has been known to survive colder temperatures, often growing back from the base if severe frosts kill the stems above ground. Cold drying winds will also brown the leaf tips so it prefers a sheltered spot in the garden, but grows well on north or east walls, which makes a nice change for a slightly tender plant.

Although attractive grow-ing through trees, (and growing up to 7m), the twining stems can cut into the tree bark over time, and its vigour can be a little excessive. It is best pruned in the spring, when long thin tendrils should be cut back to the main stems. It can be pruned to the ground, but will take at least a year before it flowers again.

There is a pale pink flowered form (*J. officinale* f. *affine* syn. *J. grandiflorum*) with 4cm flowers and two variegated leaf forms, both with white flowers. *J. beesianum* has pinkish red flowers and simple lance shaped leaves. All these are hardy to –5°C.

Jasminum officinale flowering in the author's garden in May

Passiflora

Passion Flower

Passiflora caerulea

There are some four hundred species in this genus, nearly all native to tropical America. They climb quickly by means of coiled tendrils along the stems and have lobed, dark green leaves. The flowers are striking, with the complex arrangement of petals, stamens and styles giving rise to the popular common name with the supposed resemblance to elements of Christ's crucifixion.

All the passion flowers are rampant scramblers that need the support of wires, trellis or a tree to grow to their full potential of 6m or more. They are best grown in a sheltered spot so that our autumn gales do not blow them around too much. For the more delicate varieties, it is worth deflecting some of the winter rain away from the roots with a sheet of glass or plastic, and mulching the base of the plants in cold weather. They are generally too large to protect with a cover of any sort, but the leaves usually serve as adequate protection for the stems locally. They will often regrow from the base if cut back by a severe frost, and all should be pruned in early spring to control their size in any case.

The blue passion flower, *P. caerulea* (AGM), a native of Brazil and Peru, is quite common out of doors in the Islands and is reasonably hardy (to –10°C) when sheltered by a sunny wall further north. It has flowers with white or pinkish petals and sepals and a blue corona. Although it will produce orange coloured fruits in hot summers, they are rather dry and unpalatable. '**Constance Elliott**' is a fragrant white form that is also hardy.

P. incarnata is a fully hardy species, with pale lilac flowers. It is common in eastern America where it can become invasive. The reddish-purple flowered '**Amethyst**' (AGM) and *P.* x *caeruleoracemosa* (AGM) are worth trying for their attractive flowers, but are marginally hardy, down to 0°C. *P. edulis* is the variety that produces the edible purple-brown globe fruit seen in the supermarkets. It has attractive purple flowers but is not reliably hardy in the Islands.

Other Climbers

These are well worth trying in your garden where they will do well against a sunny wall. Some, like *Eccremocarpus*, can be grown annually from seed, avoiding the need for winter protection altogether.

Akebia quinata
Chocolate Vine

This is an exotic sounding climber from East Asia that is actually fully hardy (to −15°C) although late frost may damage the early spring flowers.

The leaves usually remain on the plant all winter, and are delicate green ovals in a palmate arrangement, light green in spring, tinged with purple in the winter. The burgundy coloured flowers appear in early spring and are quite special. A long stalk appears with several cup-like male flowers about 1cm across, finishing up with the larger, and darker, female flowers at the end.

The flowering period is relatively short, up to May only, but the plant will continue to grow, and happily romp over pergolas, and up into trees without strangling them or taking over, throughout the summer.

Akebia will grow in sun and partial shade in any well drained soil and is largely pest-free. It layers very easily but is not invasive. It is a great garden performer.

Akebia quinata

Clianthus puniceus
Lobster Claw

A great climber from New Zealand that is still not common locally but it is certainly very exotic looking. The Maoris know it as Kaka Beak after the indigenous parrots and this describes the flowers beautifully. It has glossy pinnate leaves and claw-shaped red flowers up to 7cm long in clusters that appear in spring. There are also white and pink flowered versions but they are not as striking.

Clianthus puniceus (AGM) is an evergreen shrub that is best grown against a wall where it will spread to 3m. In full sun, it should survive −5°C given shelter from cold winds.

The claw-like bloom of *Clianthus puniceus*

Delairea odorata
syn. *Senecio mikanioides*
Cape Ivy

Delairia odorata scrambling through a *Fuchsia* bush

 This evergreen climber is from South Africa. It has pale green ivy-like leaves and clusters of tiny yellow flowers that are produced in late autumn. It was brought to Europe as a houseplant but has established itself outside in many areas with mild winters. It has a prodigious growth rate and will climb up hedges and trees by twining. It will also spread along the ground, extending its range by rooting into the soil as it goes along. Although only hardy to −1°C it can regrow from below ground if it is cut back by frost. It is listed as an invasive species in Hawaii and California, and has naturalised in the wild in southern England and in several locations in Jersey.

Eccremocarpus scaber
Chilean Glory Vine

This is not commonly seen around the Islands, but many gardeners are tempted to try it for the exotic flowers it produces throughout the summer.

This evergreen climbing perennial from Chile and Peru grows in forest margins and has tubular flowers that come in red, orange, yellow and cream forms. The leaves are delicate and pinnate with a tendril at the end and they are rapid climbers, looking most attractive growing through a shrub or tree. Sun and shelter from wind are important, as is a well-drained, but not dry, soil. They can be lightly pruned in spring, but are such delicate little things they rarely need it.

The red form seems hardier than the lighter colours, surviving short periods at −4°C. It is easily and quickly grown from seed.

Eccremocarpus scaber

Muehlenbeckia complexa

This is a little deciduous creeper from New Zealand that has tiny round green leaves on dark wiry stems. It is often overlooked but it is an excellent climbing plant that will cover a fence or other support quickly and form a dense mass, also working well as ground cover. Whilst it prefers full sun, it will grow in full or semi-shade.

The flowers are insignificant and it is hardy to –5°C. There is a fine example of it in the Tamarin woods at Durrell Wildlife Park in Jersey.

Muehlenbeckia complexa

Senna corymbosa

Senna corymbosa, Durrell Wildlife, Jersey

Sometimes still sold under its original name of *Cassia corymbosa* this wonderful relative of the pea is from South America. It grows as a shrub to 1.8m but can be trained against a wall with support.

It has attractive, pinnate, mid-green leaves with huge clusters of rich buttercup yellow blooms borne usually in late summer. The flowers are 2cm across and carried on erect spikes, and locally this plant seems to flower on and off all year round. An evergreen that enjoys a sunny spot in the garden, it is hardy to –5°C.

Solanum crispum
Chilean Potato Vine

Solanum crispum is a twining climber from South America with star-shaped flowers from June to October, and is closely related to the common potato. They have pale blue flowers with prominent yellow anthers and deep green leaflets. It is hardy to –5°C. If it is cut back by colder weather it will often re-grow from the base. '**Glasnevin**' (AGM) is the best form. *S. jasminoides* (syn *S. laxum*), with blue or white flowers all summer and into the autumn, is more tender and will only take temperatures down to –1°C.

Solanum crispum climbing through a pergola, Esplanade car park, Jersey

Trachelospermum asiaticum

Known as the Star Jasmine, *Trachelospermum* has similar flowers to *Jasminum*, and is self-climbing, but it is more tender, although becoming more common locally. It produces white or pale yellow flowers in the summer with a lovely scent, and has evergreen dark glossy leaves.

Originally from Japan it will survive temperatures to –6°C. *T. jasminoides* is the Confederate Jasmine found in many gardens of the Southern States of the USA, sometimes sold as *Rhynchospermum*, and hardy to –5°C.

Full sun is essential, as is protection from strong winds, and given these conditions they will grow to 7m.

The highly scented blooms of *Trachelospernum jasminoides*

Trees

Many of the trees in this section have been a part of the local landscape for such a long time that Islanders do not really think of them as 'exotic', but it is only when I looked at their origins that I realised that we are lucky to have the climate that encourages such stalwarts in our gardens. Imports from Australia, South America and the Mediterranean are found throughout all the Islands.

Embothrium coccineum in full bloom in May

Acacia

Australian Mimosa

This a huge genus of over 1,100 trees, shrubs and climbers from S. America, southern Africa and Australia. All are grown for their tiny, scented yellow flowers, produced in late winter, and decorative leaves. It is the Australian species that are generally seen in Island parks and gardens.

A. dealbata (AGM), known as Mimosa or Silver Wattle, is commonly seen in magnificent bloom around the Islands in February and March. This is the well-known variety sold by florists at Easter (most buy it in from southern France).

Mimosa is an open, evergreen tree with delicate fern-like silvery green leaves up to 12cm long. 20cm long terminal stalks are produced in the autumn and open into round fluffy little yellow flowers with a rich scent in early spring. *A. dealbata* can grow into a very large tree, some 30m high and it must be sited carefully as heavy pruning will spoil its shape, although it can be cut back lightly each year to keep it in check. It is hardy to –3°C and even lower with age.

All the mimosas prefer neutral to acidic soil and a warm spot out of the wind. They are susceptible to late frosts that can brown the flowers and foliage overnight.

A. baileyana (AGM) is similar to *A. dealbata*, except with smaller leaves (to 5cm). The cultivar '**Purpurea**', with purple young foliage, is common in many Island gardens.

A. pravissima (Ovens Wattle) has an entirely different leaf form, and is better suited to the smaller garden, growing as a shrub to a maximum of 8m. The weeping branches are covered with small triangular leaflets (known as phyllodes) and are much loved by florists. The flower form is similar to mimosa although the scent is not as strong. This is a hardier species than mimosa (to –5°C), and may be suitable for a sheltered spot in mainland gardens.

There is a large group of *A. dealbata* opposite the Shell Garden, St Brelade in Jersey and many of the public parks in the Islands have at least one specimen tree, putting on a lovely show when not much else is in flower.

Acacia pravissima

Above:
Young foliage
of *Acacia
pravissima*

Blooms of
*Acacia
dealbata*

Eucalyptus

Gum Tree

There are over five hundred species of *Eucalyptus* from Australia and the Far East, only a few of which are grown here. Known 'down under' as gum trees, they all have aromatic foliage (commonly used in preparations for blocked noses) and many have attractive bark. With the high gum content, the wood burns readily, but they regenerate remarkably quickly from forest fires in their homeland.

Eucalypts are a little unusual in that their young leaves are very different from the leaves that develop when the plant is more mature. For example, *E. gunnii* has 2-3cm oval grey leaves on new growth, but these gradually change to 8cm long lance-shaped leaves of a blue-grey colour as the plant ages. The florist's trick is to prune back a young plant annually, to a central stem, allowing fresh juvenile growth to develop each spring.

Eucalypts have petal-less flowers composed of many showy stamens, usually white or cream, and red in the case of *E. ficifolia*. They flower in summer to autumn, depending on the species.

Eucalypts are best grown as specimen plants where their attractive leaves and bark can be seen, and where they can grow unchecked. They tolerate poor, but not dry, soils and should be used more often here for their attractive blue-grey leaves and camouflage-effect bark. With regard to hardiness, eucalypts will acclimatise to cold conditions and it is best to obtain plants from a reliable supplier that has sourced the plants from cold-adapted parents.

Eucalypts need to be planted in full sun, with shelter from cold drying winds. They must also be given adequate bare soil around the base. Most of the roots are concentrated in the top 30cm of the soil and they are very sensitive to competition for water and nutrients from nearby plants, even grass, especially in the first couple of years following planting. The shallow roots can sometimes lift paving slabs if planted too close to a path.

Eucalyptus globulus juvenile foliage

The peeling bark of
Eucalyptus viminalis

All are suitable for coppicing, and can make an attractive, if not very dense, hedge with annual pruning.

E. gunnii (AGM) (Cider Gum), is fairly common in the Islands. This variety is one of the hardiest, surviving our last really cold spell (–8.7°C in 1991) with no problem. It has the typical flaking grey and cream bark of the species and can grow to impressive heights (20m+) so must be planted away from buildings, or coppiced regularly to keep it under control.

Other species that do well here are E. parviflora (AGM) (Small Leafed Gum) and E. perriniana (Spinning Gum). They are both slower growing than E. gunnii but are capable of reaching 15m under good growing conditions. The former has attractive peeling bark. The Spinning Gum has round juvenile leaves joined at the base to the stem. When dry, they remain attached to the stem, spinning around it in the wind. Both are hardy to –5°C and will usually take lower than this for short spells.

Some examples can be seen along the Railway Walk from St. Aubin, Jersey.

Ficus carica

Common Fig Tree

The Common Fig is a member of a huge genus of plants that includes the familiar Rubber Plant and Weeping Fig that we know as houseplants. The edible fig that grows so well in the Islands is a native of the eastern Mediterranean and, unlike its tropical relatives, it is hardy to –15°C.

F. carica was one of the first plants to be cultivated by humans and has long been grown as a crop plant for its fruit that can be eaten fresh or dried, and used in jam-making. The ripe fruit does not transport or keep well after picking so it is worth growing your own!

Figs are deciduous trees, producing a spreading head of large lobed leaves up to 20cm long. Locally, they are not cut back by frosts and they can grow to 4m tall and wide. They are long-lived trees when they are happy, and can live for centuries. Free-standing trees do well here if you have the space; otherwise they can be trained against a south facing wall and must be in full sun to ripen fruit. They will also grow well in a large pot as they fruit better if given a restricted root run. To mimic this in open ground, fill the planting hole with rubble. Figs grow well in our sandy soil, as a heavy wet soil tends to encourage excessive leafy growth at the expense of fruit production. They will also tolerate slightly alkaline soils.

Pear-shaped fruit develop from tiny flowers actually inside the fruit itself (technically called a 'synconium'). We usually only get one crop a year but in exceptionally hot years two crops are sometimes produced. The fruit usually takes about 12 months to mature - baby fruits no larger than 15mm long in the autumn often overwinter to form the following year's crop of fruit. Figs are ripe when the stalk bends and the fruit hangs down.

Ficus
carica

A common complaint with figs is the loss of crop from dropped-off or dry fruit. This is caused by a lack of water. Despite needing light soils, all figs should be watered when the soil becomes dry, often as early as May, and this must continue in dry spells until picking in late summer. Pot grown figs will need watering daily from May to October.

If a tree needs pruning, do it after fruiting since the fruit is carried on the previous year's wood and winter pruning would prevent a tree fruiting for that year.

'Brown Turkey' (AGM) is a common local variety: The fruit is medium to large (7cm) and copper-coloured.

The only pest problem on figs is red spider mite (*Tetranychus urticae*) in dry summers. They can be discouraged by misting or spraying the underside of the leaves (if water restrictions allow and your plant is small enough). In wet years, fig rust (*Cerotelium fici)* can cause a mottling of the leaves that can be treated with fungicide.

Quercus ilex
Holm Oak

There are over six hundred species of Oak Tree in the northern hemisphere and most are very hardy. One less hardy species, but very familiar to us in the Channel Islands, is the Holm Oak, *Quercus ilex* (AGM). It is a native of south-western Europe, and is generally hardy to –8°C, although its hardiness increases with age.

Fast growing, this tree can grow 50cm a year and reach a maximum of 25m. It grows as a rounded evergreen shrub, reaching tree proportions after twenty years. It has dark grey bark and slightly toothed shiny dark green leaves with a pale underside. These leaves are 7cm long and drop at intervals all year round. It produces short brown catkins in late spring, followed by copious stubby acorns in the autumn. These germinate readily and the Holm Oak has become widespread across the Islands, occurring in areas as diverse as windswept sand dunes and dense woodland.

They tolerate hard pruning and can be grown as a hedge, or a large topiary specimen and make a good shelter-belt in coastal locations. However, their dense shade and widespread roots prevent the growth of most other plants beneath them.

Whilst less susceptible to disease than the common oak, *Q. robur*, they are still prone to honey fungus (*Armillaria mellea* – a persistent problem in some local gardens) at any age.

Left: A crown pruned *Quercus ilex* has its overall height reduced

Other Trees

Rather less common, but still popular in local gardens, are some of the more tender plants such as the Silk Tree (*Albizia*), Tree Ferns and the Hardy Banana which all survive happily here, given the right location.

Albizia julibrissin

Silk Tree

Originally from subtropical regions of Africa and Asia, it may be a surprise that *A. julibrissin* will survive –5°C with no problem, and will survive even colder temperatures if it has had a hot summer preceding the winter to ripen the wood sufficiently.

The foliage is attractive in its own right, with 45cm long pinnate leaves with many leaflets in a fern-like bright green, that appear each spring. These are crowned in the summer by wonderful round tufts of flowers, in yellow-green, white (*A. julibrissin* var. *alba*) or pink (*A. julibrissin* var. *rosea* (AGM), each about 3cm across. The flowers usually open in July and last into August.

When fully grown, the dome-shaped tree will reach 6m, with a spread of up to 6m. It is best grown in a sunny, sheltered spot out of the wind, which could damage the delicate leaves.

There are two trees at the original entrance to the General Hospital in St. Helier, Jersey.

Albizia julibrissin var. *rosea*

Brugmansia suaveolens

Angel's Trumpet

Brugmansia is native to South America, particularly the Andes, where they grow on sloping terrain under damp conditions. They are best known for the 20cm long bell-like flowers that hang down from the plant with a fabulous scent in the late afternoon. They come in a range of colours: white, cream, yellow and pink, each flower lasting 2-3 days. *Brugmansia* are deciduous trees that are ideally suited to the Channel Island climate as they tolerate cool conditions, do not like excessively hot weather and love the rain. They will tolerate short spells at –2°C as long as the roots do not freeze.

Brugmansia suaveolens bloom

Brugmansia suaveolens

With mild winters, they will grow to 10m tall, with a spread of 5m and can even grow to 5m in a large container. They will reach these dimensions quickly, putting on 2m of growth in a season if kept very well watered and fed. They can be shy to flower in the heat; many only flower after autumn rains, which can damage the thin petals of *B. suaveolens*.

All parts of the plant are poisonous but this does not deter red spider mite and capsid bugs that love the fresh green leaves.

Sometimes *Brugmansia* are confused with *Datura* – the main difference is that *Datura* is an annual herbaceous plant (does not produce wood) and the flowers face up; *Brugmansia* is a perennial bush or tree and the flowers hang down. Both have scented blooms.

Crinodendron hookerianum

Chilean Lantern Tree

 This Chilean plant is the most fabulous tree in flower. It has small, cerise, lantern-like blooms hanging in clusters all over the plant in May and June, rather like Christmas baubles. However, it is somewhat tender, supposedly only to –5°C, although the tree pictured survived the winter of 1991 when air temperatures fell to –8.7°C in Jersey.

C. hookerianum needs a sheltered spot in full or partial sun, and acidic, well-drained soil. It will grow slowly to a tree of some 3m tall in our climate and is evergreen although the small dark leaves are sparse and it can be rather bland when not in flower. Whilst pest free, it is unfortunately susceptible to honey fungus.

Above: *Crinodendron hookerianum* flowers

Left: *Crinodendron hookerianum* in bloom

Dicksonia antarctica

Soft Tree Fern

This prehistoric looking plant is a native of Tasmania and south-eastern Australia where it grows in wooded valleys, mostly in shade and always near water. There are several genera and over six hundred different species of tree fern but *D. antarctica* is the hardiest of all. They can sometimes experience snow in their natural environment and are hardy down to –6°C. Large specimens often grow, very slowly, to 10m in their natural home. The trunks are thick and fibrous and composed of columns of roots that must be kept moist at all times, especially in the summer months. Each frond can be up to 2m long. Locally, I would recommend installing a drip irrigation system to the crown, as recent summers have been particularly warm and dry.

They need copious amounts of organic matter in the soil, especially on our light soils and heavy annual mulching to keep the roots cool. They must also be kept sheltered from strong or drying winds that will desiccate the soft foliage. See 'Hints to Keep Exotics Happy' for winter protection hints.

Dicksonia antarctica, Candie Gardens, Guernsey

Embothrium coccineum

Chilean Fire Bush

This Chilean plant is a fabulous tree in flower. It is a member of the Protea family and, like them, it needs quite acidic soils and no added phosphates. Rarely seen because it is a rather fussy plant, it will reward you well if it is planted in a sheltered woodland garden with shaded roots and moist humus-rich soil.

In May, 10cm long clusters of scarlet tubes explode into colour all over the tree, justifying its common name. *E. coccineum* is an evergreen tree with lance-shaped leaves that is hardy to –5°C. It grows to 10m tall in its native Chile, and 5m wide, but local specimens are around 7m tall. Unlike many trees, even quite young plants will produce flowers if grown in ideal conditions.

E. coccineum '**Lanceolatum**' has narrower leaves and is reliably hardier, down to –10°C with really bright orange-red flowers. In the winter, cover small trees with fleece if they are in an exposed spot, as severe weather may result in substantial leaf loss.

E. coccineum in full bloom

Fremontodendron californicum
California Glory

This is a Californian import that I would love to see more widely grown for its fantastic showy flowers. These bright yellow blooms are 4-6cm across and borne from May through to September. The five calyces (there are no petals) are shaped like wide yellow saucers and remain open for several days. It is reputed to be tender, but can certainly tolerate the occasional low of −10°C when planted in a sunny location. The felt-like grey-green lobed leaves are rather sparse, although evergreen.

Grow *Fremontodendron* in a sheltered south facing position in well-drained soil, preferably against a wall and the reflected heat will produce the best show of flowers. It grows slowly to 7m tall by 5m wide against a wall, and it will grow as a shrub too. It enjoys the dry soil at the base of a house wall and the small root system poses no problem to the foundations.

It has downy hair covering the shoots and leaves that can be irritating to some people. Bigger problems may arise from the fine spines covering the seed capsules. These capsules can fall off, unnoticed, onto your lawn, for unsuspecting bare feet to tread on! Please don't let this put you off, this really is a superb plant.

Above:
Fremontodendron californicum reaches into a sunny sky, author's garden, Jersey

Left:
The bright yellow *Fremontodendron* bloom

Musa basjoo
Japanese Hardy Banana

A banana plant, whilst not really a tree, is the essential 'must have' for a tropical look in any garden. It is one of my favourite plants and it always amazes visitors that we can grow banana plants this far north.

M. basjoo (AGM) produces huge apple-green leaves up to 2m long at a rate of one a week at the height of the summer and eventually a succulent purple trunk will form. Grown in the soil and given a lot of water and a good high-nitrogen feed, it will eventually reach 4m tall if undamaged by frosts.

Mature plants will produce fruit; swollen dark orange bracts unfold to reveal yellow flowers, behind which develop small (green and inedible!) fruit in hot summers. This stem will die after fruiting, but new shoots will arise from the base and these can be left to form a clump, if you have the space.

Frost will destroy the foliage, but the stem will tolerate –3°C for short periods before it too collapses. The plant is root hardy but the stem can be wrapped in hessian or woven fleece to protect it against chilly winds. Despite its hardiness, the delicate sail-like leaves are easily ripped by strong winds.

Olea europaea
Olive Tree

A Mediterranean native, *O. europaea* (AGM) is hardy to –7°C. It is becoming more popular in the Islands. It is particularly attractive in a large terracotta pot where it will grow happily for several years if watered well in the summer. The small (8cm) grey-green leaves, with a paler underside, are quite distinctive. Small white flowers appear in the summer, sometimes followed by edible green fruit if the summer and autumn are sufficiently hot.

They need sharply drained soil and full sun to achieve their potential height of 10m.

Olea europaea

Hedges

One of the main characteristics of the Channel Islands' climate is the almost persistent wind, with windless days being rare. South-westerly winds of Force 6-8 (25-40mph) are common in the winter months. While this can keep the temperatures mild, it means that local gardeners need effective hedges to provide some shelter in exposed gardens. As these winds are usually salt-laden, plants that are tolerant to such abuse are the most popular. The following are some shrubs useful as hedges in the Islands.

Fuchsia magellanica

Elaeagnus

This genus has over forty species, largely from Asia, and all are fully hardy in Britain. Their popularity locally stems from their tolerance of dry soil conditions and windy coastal locations. *Eleagnus* have alternate, lance- shaped leaves about 5-7cm in length, and small, tubular, creamy flowers in the autumn and into the winter. These often have a fantastic scent that has passers-by looking around for something more flamboyant! Edible silvery-red berries, some 2cm in length, then follow in the spring, and are popular with birds.

Showing a preference for acidic soils, all *Eleagnus* grow well in sun, and the evergreen types will do well in partial shade too. Many of the varieties grown here are the more decorative variegated types, and all of these can throw out plain green shoots that must be cut out to avoid the whole plant gradually reverting to the more vigorous green form. All are quite fast growing; they put on some 45cm annually with lots of whippy young shoots growing even more than that.

For a dense hedge, plant 60cm young plants between 45-60cm apart. They make neat hedges up to 2m tall and 1m wide and are very tolerant of pruning if a smaller hedge is required.

E. x *ebbingei* cultivars are evergreen with 10cm leathery leaves with a silvery lower surface. Attractive variegated varieties include '**Gilt Edge**' (AGM) – leaves have dark green centres with large yellow margins, and '**Limelight**' with yellow and pale green leaves. *E.* x *ebbingei* prefers a well-drained soil, and, once established, is very drought resistant and will succeed in quite dry soils.

E. macrophylla (a parent of the above) and *E. pungens,* both evergreen, are also found on the Islands. *E. pungens* has many variegated types; '**Maculata**' (AGM) has bright yellow centres to the leaves and '**Variegata**' has narrow yellow margins around a green centre.

All are hardy to −15°C and probably lower but some leaf loss will occur then. They are pest free and show some tolerance to honey fungus

Eleagnus x *ebbingei* '**Limelight**'

Escallonia rubra

Escallonia
'Apple Blossom'

There are sixty species in this genus, mostly evergreen shrubs from mountainous regions of South America. They grow well on dry, sandy loams and are very tolerant of extreme maritime exposure. They have small, oval, glossy, dark green (and slightly sticky) leaves and clusters of small pink to white flowers that appear throughout the year. Most species are only frost-hardy to –10°C

There are some hardy species, and the commonest here is *E. rubra*, which is very vigorous, usually grown as a hedge to some 4m, and hardy to –15°C. In exceptional cold the plant may lose a lot of leaf. Cold, drying wind is more an enemy as the leaves can get scorched under these conditions but they usually recover.

The bees adore the flowers, which have a slight scent, and a hedge in full bloom is a wonderful sight. There are many examples all over the Islands as *Escallonia* is well suited to our light soils and sunny summer conditions. They need an annual or biannual prune in early spring and again after flowering if the hedge is getting too wide, and they will also tolerate a more severe pruning when growth starts in the spring, if they are in danger of outgrowing their allotted space – they can grow to 2.5m wide as well as high. They resent transplanting so should be planted in their final positions as soon as possible.

For a dense hedge, plant 60cm young plants between 45-60cm apart. They make a neat hedge that will grow up to 30cm a year.

The deep pink flowers of *E. rubra* **'Crimson Spire'** (AGM) are 2cm long and produced all summer long. Other popular local species include *E.* **'Apple Blossom'** (AGM) that has light pink flowers and forms a dense hedge, some 2.5m high, but is less hardy (to –7°C), as is *E.* **'Pride of Donard'** (AGM) with deep pink flowers.

Griselinia littoralis

An introduction from New Zealand, this plant makes a superb evergreen hedge in the Islands because of its tolerance of coastal conditions. *G. littoralis* will withstand temperatures down to –10°C although it is happier in our warmer climate and grows best in full sun. In well-drained soil it will grow to a shrub of some 8m by 5m if left unpruned. However, it is rather slower growing than the previous two hedge shrubs, taking some years to form a thick hedge from a 50cm young plant. It does transplant well however, so larger plants can be used to make a hedge more quickly. It is notably resistant to honey fungus.

It has 10cm long oval leaves that are a lovely shiny apple-green colour. It has inconspicuous yellow flowers in the spring but will only produce the purple fruit if both sexes are present.

Griselinia will form a dense hedge from young plants planted 60cm apart and although usually kept below this, a height of 2m is possible. Annual growth is in the region of 30cm a year and pruning once a year is enough to keep the hedge tidy.

The plain green form is the most common and very attractive, but '**Variegata**' (AGM) has leaves with cream margins and streaks, and '**Dixon's Cream**' has cream centres, if a more colourful hedge is required. There is a lovely hedge of green *Griselinia* near the teahouse in Candie Gardens, Guernsey.

Griselinia littoralis, Candie Gardens, Guernsey

Laurus nobilis

Bay Tree

Another Mediterranean import, and also common in the Canaries and Azores, this shrub has numerous uses. In ancient times it made up the wreath worn by Roman emperors and Grecian sportsmen. Nowadays Bay is grown for the aromatic 10cm long leaves that can be used whole in soups and stews and as an ingredient in 'Bouquet Garni'. It is grown as a hedge in many gardens as it is a fast growing evergreen with glossy dark green leaves. It also responds well to clipping and makes attractive large topiary specimens.

Bay is common in all the Islands, often used as hedging but it is not good as a windbreak because it is susceptible to browning of the leaves on the coasts, or when the wind is particularly cold. It likes moist, well-drained, fertile soil in sun or light shade. It is hardy to −10°C, and probably lower as it re-grows readily from the base if cut back. It is fast growing, reaching a mature height of 12m with a 10m spread at a rate of up to 1m a year if it is not pruned annually. For a dense hedge, plant 60cm tall young plants about 45cm apart.

In climates colder than ours, bay trees can be difficult to over-winter. In pot specimens, withholding water in late summer and early autumn can help to induce semi-dormancy but this isn't always possible for plants in the ground.

Bay produces small yellow flowers in the spring and, if you have male and female plants, easily sets small, black, egg-shaped berries. These will sprout rapidly around the garden and have very tenacious roots, even as a seedling, so must be removed quickly.

While generally free from pests and diseases, in some years the bay sucker (*Trioza alacris*) can cause considerable leaf curling. The only control is to remove any affected leaves and dispose of them.

L. nobilis (AGM) is the commonest species, but there are many forms as it hybridises easily and some have better flavour for cooking; others have smooth or crinkly edges to the leaves.

Laurus nobilis foliage

Pittosporum

This is a great Australasian import, with over two hundred species that grow in habitats ranging from rain forest through to savannah. Despite this, only two species are common locally; *P. tenuifolium* from New Zealand and *P. tobira* from south-east Asia.

P. tenuifolium (AGM) is commonly seen as a hedge where its tough leaves cope well with our windy climate. The young stems are black with wavy-edged shiny green leaves, 6cm long. The flowers are almost black in colour with a honey-like scent and appear for a few short weeks in late April in the Islands. The stems are popular as long-lasting cut foliage in the floristry trade.

The dark flowers of *Pittosporum tenuifolium*

P. tenuifolium grows quickly when young (60cm a year) and can be planted every 75cm for a quick hedge, or up to 1.5m apart if a larger hedge is required. It responds well to an annual pruning and can be cut back quite severely if needed. As a single specimen plant it will grow into a rounded shrub up to 8m tall, and 3m wide.

There are many varieties with several variegated or bronze-leafed types that are particularly attractive. All *P. tenuifolium* are hardy to –8°C although there may be leaf loss in especially cold spells. They are usually pest and disease free.

P. tobira (AGM), also known as the Japanese Mock Orange, is the second species that grows well in the Channel Islands. It is usually grown for the sweetly scented flowers that appear during early summer, and indeed, can appear on and off throughout the growing season. Yellow seed capsules follow these in the autumn. The leaves are smooth and mid-green, up to 10cm long and

Pittosporum '**Garnettii**'

borne in whorls on strong upright stems.

This plant makes a fine hedge with good salt and wind resistance, perfect for our rather windy location, and can take the occasional heavy pruning. It is hardy to –7° C. It can be planted the same distance apart as *P. tenuifolium* but is slower growing, at only 20cm a year. The older leaves can turn yellow and drop off in the spring before the new growth starts, but this is perfectly normal and the plant can be pruned back to prevent it becoming too leggy.

P. tobira will produce more flowers in full sunshine, but the foliage looks better in light shade. It has good drought tolerance when established, due to the thick leathery leaves, and should be more widely grown. The only pest problem is the black aphid that loves the new leaves and flowers. A quick spray with diluted washing-up liquid will get rid of them before they distort the developing leaves.

P. tobira **'Variegatum'** (AGM) has beautiful silvery makings on the leaves and is slightly less hardy (–5°C) than the species.

The variegated form of *Pittosporum tobira*

Other Hedges

Fuchsia

These plants originate from Central and South America and New Zealand and there are over 8,000 hybrids and cultivars available. They are commonly grown as shrubs and colourful, airy hedges and are widely planted throughout the Channel Islands.

If you are used to seeing the plants everywhere you may not have realised that many *Fuchsia* species are only hardy down to –5°C with very few fully hardy at –15°C. Locally the woody stems are permanent and they are in flower from May through to December, even continuing to flower after many of the leaves have fallen off in the autumn.

Most *Fuchsia* have pendant flowers with a skirt of 4 sepals, surrounding a 'petticoat' of petals (collectively known as a corolla), often of differing colours, and all feature a protruding stigma and stamens. All local species are deciduous shrubs with simple lance-shaped leaves.

Fuchsia will grow in sun or partial shade in most soil types, but prefer protection from drying winds, especially in the winter. Wait until all danger of frosts has passed before pruning down to newly emerging leaves. Here we can prune quite severely if a bush has grown too large, right down to 30cm above ground, and the resulting growth will often exceed 100cm in a season.

Garden pests include capsid bugs, which can completely destroy the flowering shoot in some years, and whitefly. Keep an eye out for these from May onwards.

Hedge Varieties

The best *Fuchsia* hedges locally are of *Fuchsia magellanica* (often synonymous with *F.* **'Riccartonii'**). They have dark green leaves with a slight bronze sheen and small (4cm long) single flowers. These have scarlet sepals and a purple corolla and are produced in profusion from June right into December. The flowers look fantastic *en masse* and a hedge will grow up to 3m tall in sheltered areas. It is hardy to –10°C.

Other varieties that happily form a shorter hedge, up to 1.5m, are **'Phyllis'** (AGM), a semi-double with cerise red sepals and a rose red corolla and **'Mrs Popple'** (AGM), a hardy scarlet and violet variety.

The exotic-looking *fuchsia* **'Thalia'**

Fuchsia **'Mrs Popple'**

Shrub Varieties

There are numerous other varieties that develop into reliably hardy shrubs here in the Channel Islands. These two will cope with temperatures to –7°C; **'Dollar Princess'** (AGM) has cerise sepals and a double purple corolla, growing to 45cm tall. **'Garden News'** (AGM) grows to 60 cm with double flowers of icy pink sepals and a magenta corolla. My favourite for an exotic look is **'Thalia'** (AGM), a member of the Triphylla group with long tubular orange flowers and purple tinted leaves. It is stunningly tropical in appearance, growing to 90cm, but is only hardy to around +1°C and is best pot grown to allow winter protection, even locally.

Olearia

Daisy Bush

Olearia is a big group of plants with 130 species that include small trees and shrubs. All originate from Australasia and occur naturally in a wide range of habitats from coastal bogs to mountain scrub.

This attractive plant is known as the Daisy Bush due to the typical daisy form of the flowers, commonly white, with a delicate fragrance. It has glossy evergreen leaves and grows well in mild, wet and windy areas – perfect for the Channel Islands!

The flowers appear from early spring to summer, above deep green leaves. It flowers best following a long hot summer the previous year, and it appreciates a warm spot in the garden, with well-drained soil. It will also succeed on chalk.

Olearia respond well to hard pruning, but annual light pruning should be carried out after flowering. It is generally pest and disease free.

Olearia traversii is a common species on the Islands and it makes a good coastal hedge because it is salt tolerant and fast growing, putting on up to 1.5 m a year. It is best kept under 3m but will grow into a 6m tree if left unpruned. It is hardy to –12°C. *Olearia macrodonta* (AGM) is a vigorous variety with holly-like leaves, also widely grown, with **'Minor'** the more dwarf form.

Olearia macrodonta in bloom in June

Tamarix tetrandra

Tamarisk

This shrub is well suited to the light sandy soils of the Islands, and is totally unaffected by the salt-laden gales that frequently sweep in from the west. Although a fully hardy shrub from south-east Europe, tamarisk is often used as a hedge in our coastal gardens, and the sea front of St Aubin's Bay in Jersey has several such hedges. These are cut back annually to keep them at a height of only 1m or so.

T. tetrandra develops plumes of small pink flowers in late spring that appear before the needle-like leaves. Some will develop into small trees but they are usually grown as a small shrub of 1m x 1m.

They need full sun and a well-drained soil, particularly if they are susceptible to occasional flooding by seawater. They also need regular pruning to avoid becoming top heavy and woody at the base, and can be cut back to 30-40 cm each year after flowering.

T. pentandra (syn. *T. ramosissima*) has pink flowers that appear in late summer above feathery foliage on reddish branches.

Tamarix tetrandra, grown as a tree, St. Helier, Jersey

Shrubs & Perennials

The following pages include a host of shrubs and perennial plants that enjoy the mild winters and high sunshine hours that the Islands receive in the summer months. It was particularly hard to narrow down this section to a few choice plants as there are many that thrive in our mild climate. Perhaps the most well known are the tall blue globes of *Agapanthus* that are found in many gardens throughout all the Islands.

Callistemon citrinus

Agapanthus

African Lily

Agapanthus is probably the most widely planted 'exotic' grown in the Channel Islands. Garden centres often sell out of the plants in July as few gardeners can resist the great blue globes of flowers, rising several feet above a mass of green leaves. For visitors, they, together with the *Cordyline* 'palms', seem to be the epitome of our more favourable climate. Like many of the exotic plants of the Channel Islands, they are natives of southern Africa, having been introduced during the 17th century and have been widely grown here ever since.

The species commonly seen is likely to be a hybrid of several *Agapanthus africanus* types, rather than one pure species, as they hybridise and set seed readily. However, all have long, strap-like leaves, amongst which rise tall, sturdy stems, each topped by a ball of dozens of tubular flowers in the summer.

Originally from coastal South Africa, they need warm, sunny positions on well-drained soil. Whilst they should be given plenty of water in dry summers, they dislike winter wet. They do exceptionally well in a large container too, which can be moved into a frost-free shed if necessary over winter. Pot specimens must never dry out or they will not flower well the following year.

There are about ten species of this perennial plant, broadly divided into evergreens such as *A. africanus* (AGM) with wide leaves, and deciduous types like *A. campanulatus,* with narrower leaves and flared flowers. The evergreens originate from the warmer areas of South Africa, and overwinter happily here, tolerating temperatures as low as –5°C. Away from the coasts of mainland Britain it may be preferable to chose one of the many *A. campanulatus* varieties that, especially if mulched and not kept too wet, will cope with the hardest of British winters (to –15°C).

A. campanulatus has given rise to the best choice of varieties. '**Headbourne Hybrids**' are a group originally raised in the UK by the Honourable Lewis Palmer during the 1950s. This small, relatively hardy, deciduous *Agapanthus* is still available in a wide range of colours. However, the name has been misapplied to cover a range of variable seedlings so buy from reputable sources.

In fact, there are now so many *Agapanthus* varieties available that the RHS lists over four hundred, with flower colours from pure white, through cream, pale blue and lilac to the deepest midnight blue. There is even one with variegated leaves. Heights also vary, from miniature forms like '**Peter Pan**' (30cm) and '**Tinkerbell**' (50cm) to giants like '**Buckingham Palace**' (180cm) with heads as big as footballs. I like the unusual *A. praecox* '**Flore Pleno**' with double blue flowers. All look spectacular planted in large drifts, if you have the space, or in terracotta pots on a sunny patio.

Above: The delicate blue of an *Agapanthus* bloom

Left: *Agapanthus africanus*

Below: *Agapanthus africanus*, Les Vaux, Jersey

Callistemon citrinus

Bottlebrush

The popular name for this genus of 25 shrubs from Australia derives from the distinctive bright, often red, flowers that appear in cylindrical tufts, up to 15cm long, at the end of branches. Individual blooms have prominent stamens that give the brush-like effect. The branches continue to grow after the flowers have formed, with new leaves appearing at the tips. The seed capsules remain attached to the branches like hard brown peas as the stem continues to grow.

The narrow evergreen leaves are greyish-green on upright, or gracefully drooping, branches. Given their origin, they require full sun and a dry location to ensure the best flowers and do particularly well in front of our granite walls where they receive lots of reflected heat. Other colours are available, but it is the red forms that are generally seen around the Islands.

In their native Australia *Callistemon* grow alongside streams and riverbeds so although they need a free-draining but moisture retentive, acidic soil they dislike waterlogging. They are also tolerant of salt-laden winds.

Callistemon will tolerate hard pruning, but they do not usually need any as they reach a maximum height of only 2m under local conditions and are well suited to small gardens. They are usually pest-free when grown outside.

Bottlebrushes are really worth growing to lend a tropical air to the garden. Usually seen in reds and pinks, lemon-flowered forms are also available.

The common local variety is *C. citrinus* **'Splendens'** (AGM) with bright red bottle-brushes in June and July and broad leaves. It is hardy to –6°C. Hardier still is *C. rigidus* with deep red flowers. *C. sieberi* (AGM) is the hardiest of all the species; surviving occasional lows of –15°C; it has creamy yellow flowers. *C. pallidus* (Lemon Bottle-brush) has 10cm long greenish-yellow spikes but is only hardy to –5°C.

Howard Davis Park, Jersey, and Sausmarez Manor, Guernsey, have some nice red varieties.

Callistemon citrinus

Ceanothus

Californian Lilac

The Islands can be a riot of blue shades in May, hot (or rather cool) on the heels of the reds and pinks of the camellias in early spring. This is down to the many Californian Lilac shrubs planted locally. The colours range from dark purple to bright lilac.

Most *Ceanothus* flower for a few short weeks in May, but are useful evergreens all year round, with glossy deep-green foliage. They have a reputation for being slightly tender, coming as they do from the sunshine States of California and Oregon in the south-western USA. However, they do well if grown with the shelter and warmth offered by a sunny south-facing wall. They like deep, acidic soil and need full sun.

Ceanothus is a hungry plant that responds well to an annual dose of general fertiliser in the spring that will boost flowering and new growth. They flower on last season's wood so only prune lightly after flowering, if necessary.

There is a basic division of *Ceanothus* into two groups and both types are best planted

in spring to give them a full season's growth before the winter sets in:

• Most *Ceanothus* are evergreen and these are generally the less hardy types which need the shelter of one of our warm granite walls. They have small, dark green glossy leaves and small clusters of tiny flowers. Most are upright shrubs that will grow up to 3m and many are happiest above –6°C. The May flowering *C. thyrsiflorus* (which grows wild around San Francisco) is common locally. *C. arboreus* **'Trewithen Blue'** (AGM) has large leaves and is more tender, only tolerating the occasional low of –5°C. It has large bunches of powder blue flowers and can grow to 6m in a sheltered spot.

• The deciduous group is hardier (to –15°C) and will grow in a sunny spot in most areas of the mainland as well as locally. The leaves tend to be larger with bigger, looser, clusters of flowers, but the shrub remains about 2m tall and wide. They bloom in late summer and *C.* x *delileanus* **'Gloire de Versailles'**, (AGM) with its sky blue flowers, is the most popular.

Above: Pale blue *Ceanothus* flowering in early May
Left: *Ceanothus arboreus* **'Trewithen Blue'**

Cistus

Rock Rose

This Mediterranean classic grows here almost at its northern boundary and it is, in general, not particularly hardy, with harsh winters below around –6°C killing it entirely.

Known as Rock (or Sun) Roses, this common name has also been applied to the closely related *Helianthemum* (all below 30cm in height and hardy) *Halimium* and the hybrid *Halimiocistus*. True *Cistus* are all pink or white; yellow and cream shades only occur in these other genera.

Cistus form a rounded evergreen bush with silvery-green felt-like (and sometimes sticky) leaves and delicate flowers like crumpled tissue paper, about 6cm across. The flowers are short-lived, opening in the morning and dropping the petals at night. However, fresh flowers replace these each morning and a healthy shrub will be in flower from June to August.

The plants do well on the light sandy soil near our coasts and do not mind maritime locations but they do object to a windy site as they have brittle branches. It is particularly important to avoid wet sites that are responsible for the death of more *Cistus* than winter cold alone. The plants don't need any pruning, and usually do not regrow from cut back shoots. Old bushes can get tall and woody and are best replaced.

All *Cistus* are slow growing, and most have a distinctive scent. This is due to a viscous substance, exuded on hot summer days, called ladanum. This ladanum is used in the manufacture of incense and perfume and forms part of the Holy Oil of the Greek Orthodox Church. It

has been collected from *Cistus* plants since antiquity.

The tallest species tend to be the hardiest; these include *C.* x *cyprius* (AGM) with large white flowers and a wine blotch at the base of each petal, and *C. laurifolius* with white flowers. Both grow to 2m, have sticky green leaves and are hardy to –15°C.

The shorter *C.* '**Grayswood Pink**' (AGM) is very hardy (to –15°C). It is often confused with *C.* x *argenteus* '**Peggy Sammons**' (AGM), *C.* x *argenteus* '**Silver Pink**' and *C.* x *skanbergii* (AGM), all of which have pink flowers and grow to around 1m. These three are only hardy to –5°C but are common throughout the Islands.

The delicate pink flowers of *Cistus* x *pulverulentus* '**Sunset**' in the author's garden

Convolvulus cneorum

Silver Bush

This is not the invasive climbing bindweed that gardeners dread, but an unusual shrubby member of the same genus. It is a native of Mediterranean limestone hills, and enjoys a hot sunny position in a rock garden, where soil fertility is fairly low and drainage is good.

The evergreen foliage is covered in silky silver-grey hairs, and the flowers start as pink buds, which open into 2.5cm (1in) trumpets, with bluish white petals marked with a central pink stripe on the reverse. It flowers at intervals from May to August and dead-heading helps promote a longer succession of flowers.

C. cneorum makes an attractive plant that benefits from annual pruning after flowering to maintain bushy growth, keeping it around 60cm high. It is best grown in full sun in any well-drained soil where it provides great ground cover. It hates waterlogging and can be short-lived in wet conditions, but will tolerate –10°C on a sharply drained soil out of cold winds.

Convolvulus cneorum in an arid border, Coronation Park, Jersey

Hebe

This is a large genus of shrubs from New Zealand, and it is in the same family as *Veronica* with very similar looking flower spikes.

They are not as tender as they were once thought to be, with many actually very hardy and quite happy in our salt-laden air. The whipcord types have leaves held very close to the stem and are the hardiest, but with very small flowers. Larger leaved varieties have bigger flowers and are usually less cold tolerant and it is these varieties that are common in gardens throughout the Channel Islands.

All *Hebe* have flowers at the pink-to-blue end of the colour spectrum (or white) in terminal spires at the end of the many shoots and they flower freely between May and November, depending on the variety. The common varieties have elliptic dark green leaves, often on purplish stems, with flowers spikes from 3 to 7cm long. They can vary in height from ground cover varieties like the white *H. chathamica* at 15cm tall to the lilac *H.* '**Midsummer Beauty**' (AGM) at 2m tall. Both of these are hardy to –6°C.

The medium height *Hebe* '**Autumn Glory**' is common locally, growing to 60cm tall with violet flowers in bloom from June to November. *H. albicans* (AGM) has pure white flowers in early summer. Both are reliably hardy to –5°C.

Taller varieties that do well locally are *Hebe* '**Mrs. Winder**' (AGM) that grows to 1m with violet blue flowers. *H.* '**Great Orme**' (AGM), at 1.2m, has bright pink flowers from July to October. Both are reliably hardy to –5°C. *H. salicifolia* is well suited to hedging in our milder climate. It will grow to a height and spread of 2.5m with lilac-tipped white flowers from June to September. It is fully hardy to –15°C.

All *Hebe* are easy to grow plants that enjoy a well-drained soil in full sun or partial shade. They prefer only lightly fertile soils and will tolerate slightly alkaline conditions. Pruning is not usually necessary as there is such a range of forms that a variety can usually be found to fill any space in the garden.

The delicate flower spikes of *Hebe* attract insects

Other Shrubs and Perennials

There are many other shrubs, such as the Mediterranean oleander, that are guaranteed to add a touch of the tropics to local gardens. In addition, the sandy soil and mild climate allows herbs such as lavender and rosemary to grow all year round and the latter is frequently used as a shrub in public landscaping. Common to all is their need for well-drained soil in a sunny corner of the garden.

Abelia x grandiflora

Abelia x *grandiflora* flowers

Abelia is an attractive shrub with a graceful habit, pleasant foliage and pretty funnel-shaped flowers. They are members of the honeysuckle family with some 15 species found in China, Japan and Mexico.

Many species are not reliably hardy in cool temperate regions, but some do well in our mild climate. *Abelia* x *grandiflora* (AGM) is the hardiest and will survive temperatures down to –6°C and possibly more if it is in a sheltered spot. It is an upright shrub, growing to about 2m wide and tall. *Abelia* flowers on the current year's growth, with blooms appearing from mid-summer well into the autumn. It has white flowers tinged with pink and russet 5-pointed calyces that remain attractive long after the flowers have fallen. In the Islands it is semi-deciduous with many leaves being retained over the winter and it enjoys our free-draining soil. It will grow in sun or partial shade, as long as it is out of the wind.

Relatively pest free, this plant will also take a hard pruning in the early spring, if it gets too large, and it is a real gem that should be more widely planted.

Cyperus alternifolius

Umbrella Grass

Cyperus alternifolius is one of several species of ornamental grass-like plants that are used to provide height along the edges of garden ponds. *C. alternifolius* is reliably hardy in the Channel Islands once established. A cold (sub-zero) wind will dry and bleach the leaves, but new shoots will appear in profusion once the weather warms up. It is a native of Madagascar and will grow up to 2m tall in a sheltered spot where it has access to plenty of water. However, it will also grow quite adequately in normal soil as long as it has an unrestricted root run and the roots are kept shaded. It will remain in a neat clump, only spreading gradually to around 1m after many years. It has stiff triangular stems, topped with a cluster of grass-like leaves, and brown tufted flowers. Despite the stiff stems, they can be blown over in some of our gales and are best grown through a hoop for additional support.

Cyperus alternifolius, author's garden

Fatsia japonica
(syn. *Aralia japonica*)

Right: *Fatsia japonica*

Below: *Fatsia japonica* flowers in November, in the author's garden

Fatsia japonica (AGM) is a plant for a shady site in coastal locations as it tolerates salty air and north-facing walls although it is at home in full sun. It has large glossy palmate leaves all year round and, in the autumn, umbels of globular cream flowers appear above the foliage that last into the spring. Whilst not common, I have included it because it is hardier than most people realise and lends an unmistakably tropical air to any garden with its large leaves. It is often sold in garden centres as a houseplant,

for which it is suitable for only a short period of time as it can grow to over 3m tall and wide. Harden off indoor-grown *Fatsia* before planting outside. Knowledgeable garden centres will provide outdoor-grown specimens, able to cope with the –7°C to which it is tolerant.

The variegated varieties have cream edges to the leaves, and are much less hardy than the straight green. There is a very large green *Fatsia* near the Orang-utan enclosure, Durrell Wildlife, Jersey.

Geranium maderense
Giant Herb Robert

Geranium maderense

This tender species of Geranium has become more common in the Islands in recent years, probably brought here by Madeirans as a memory of home, and encouraged by our recent mild winters.

It is best treated as a short-lived perennial whereby it will develop a large mass of finely divided green leaves in its early years, spreading up to 1m wide. Subsequently, it produces a large spray of pink flowers with darker centres in late spring. It then usually dies but self sows seed very easily and there are often many youngsters growing up around it to continue the show in later years. These babies should be transplanted while young as they develop a big tap root. This fascinating plant folds down the older leaf stalks to touch the ground, acting as supports for the flower stems that can be up to 1m tall.

It is just about hardy in the Channel Islands, coping with temperatures down to –2°C. *G. palmatum*, from the Canaries, is taller, with less divided palmate leaves, deep pink flowers and is slightly hardier, to –3°C. Vine weevil and slugs are a common problem on both species.

Grevillea

A large genus in the Protea family, *Grevillea* are native to Australia. Many will only tolerate temperatures down to 0°C but some tolerate –7°C if the preceding summer has been hot enough to ripen the wood.

Local species include *G. rosmarinifolia* (AGM) that is generally hardy to –5°C. It is a many branched shrub growing to 2m tall and 3m wide in local conditions. It has clusters of 4cm long needle-like leaves with rolled-under margins like rosemary, and pink spider-like flowers throughout the winter. My favourite is *G.* **'Canberra Gem'** (AGM) with spiky 3cm long leaves and 5cm wide deep pink flowers that appear throughout the year, but especially from December onwards. It is wonderful to have such an exotic plant flowering in the depths of winter and it should be more widely grown.

It needs full sun for most of the day and a well-drained, neutral to acidic soil. Once established, it is reasonably drought tolerant. There are some large *Grevillea* in Coronation Park, Jersey.

Grevillea **'Canberra Gem'** in the author's garden

Leptospermum

Tea Tree

The New Zealand Tea Tree is a very attractive shrub when in flower and it is becoming more common in garden centres. It is ideal for the Channel Islands, demanding lime-free acidic soils and warm summers.

Leptospermum is a small evergreen shrub with white or pink flowers and reddish stems that produce a mass of delicate 5-petalled flowers in May and occasionally much earlier. They have neat aromatic leaves and frequently softly hairy stems. They grow to about 2m and look lovely planted in groups of three or five in herbaceous borders where the early flowers remind us that summer is on its way. They will even suit a low hedge.

L. rupestre (AGM) is the hardiest (to −10°C), producing a white-flowered prostrate shrub some 1m tall by 1.5m wide. *L. scoparium* is more common (and hardy to −5°C), with many different cultivars with flowers from white through to dark pink. It grows to 3m.

Leptospermum scoparium in flower

Lavandula

Lavender

This plant is ideally suited to the predominant soil type in many areas of the Channel Islands, as it loves a sandy, very well-drained soil that can be low in nutrients.

Lavenders originate from the Mediterranean and thrive in periods of drought, and although it can grow in a wide range of soils, all of these need to be well-drained because the plant will not tolerate sitting in cold, wet soil through the winter. Planting in full sun is also essential to get the best flower performance.

Lavender plants can look good for up to twenty years if they are pruned at the right time. *L. augustifolia* needs to be cut back to 20cm after flowering in mid-August. By the end of September it will have put on a further 3cm of new growth, or more if the weather is good. Later pruning can leave the plants vulnerable to winter weather. Regular dead-heading will promote further flushes of flowers. If using the flowers for pot-pourri or in dried arrangements, cut them before the blooms have fully opened to avoid petal drop. Lavenders can get leggy and woody with age if they have been neglected and it is usually unsuccessful to try to rejuvenate an old plant.

There are over 25 species and lots more cultivars of lavender with colours ranging from white, through pink to a host of blues and purples. Some varieties can be tender and should be kept in pots to be brought in to a cool place once temperatures drop below 5°C.

The variety with really good garden performance is *Lavandula augustifolia* **'Hidcote'** (AGM). This variety (hardy to −15°C) has dense, dark violet flowers borne on 30cm long stems. It is 60cm tall in flower and spreads to 75cm. *Lavandula* x *intermedia* varieties have a more robust fragrance, but they tend to be taller. *L. stoechas* (AGM) is known as French Lavender and has conspicuous coloured bracts at the top of each flower spike. The latter two tolerate temperatures down to −5°C only.

Cuckoo spit beetle (frog hopper) (*Philaenus spumarius*) is the main pest and these are best dealt with by washing off with soapy water. Honey fungus can also kill bushes at any age.

One of the National Plant Collections of *Lavandula* is held at the Jersey Lavender Farm, in St Brelade. The collection is well worth a visit, particularly during June when the scent is fantastic and harvesting for the many lavender oil products is being carried out.

Field of *Lavendula*, The Lavender Farm, Jersey

Nerium oleander

Oleander

Oleanders are Mediterranean natives and instantly evoke an exotic feel when planted in our local gardens, because they remind us of holidays in southern France and Italy.

They are erect, evergreen shrubs with stiff, lance-shaped leaves (around 12cm long) and clusters of white, pink, purple, apricot or red flowers that may be single or double and each up to 5cm wide. Even in our climate oleanders are fast growing and can reach up to 6m but are usually seen here around 3m tall, forming a rounded mound about 3m wide. Oleanders are resistant to salty winds and prolonged drought and they tolerate alkaline soils. They must be planted in well-drained soil as they dislike winter wet and and also do well in a large pot, which can be moved onto a terrace for the summer.

Oleanders need hot sun for good flowering, and they can be shy to flower in cool summers; flowering usually starts here in July and continues into September. Annual pruning after the first flush of flowers will prevent them from becoming leggy.

There are many named varieties available and an exceptional collection of these is held at a nursery in Meze, France. White varieties seem to be the fastest and tallest growing. Pink and red types are the hardiest, generally to –5°C with '**Little Red**' hardy to –12°C. The 'dwarf' '**Petite Salmon**' grows to 2m.

Oleanders are susceptible to aphid, but I have found red spider mite to be more of a problem when the weather is hot and dry. Misting the plant regularly keeps the numbers down. Yellow leaves are often the result of iron deficiency.

Being evergreen, the leaves drop off at intervals throughout the year. Dispose of leaves and clippings carefully and wear gloves when handling them, as all parts of the plant are very poisonous. Not a plant for a home with young children or animals perhaps, but very pretty and a real performer in our mild climate.

Nerium oleander '**Petite Salmon**'

Phygelius

Cape Fuchsia

This is a delightful shrub with brightly coloured flowers reminiscent of *Fuchsia* '**Thalia**' and hardier too. Originally from the Cape region of South Africa, it has a reputation for being delicate, but thrives in local gardens.

The two species, and their hybrid, are grown as semi-evergreen shrubs to 1.5 m height and spread. They have lance-shaped, dark green leaves and panicles of hanging tubular flowers with flared tips, commonly in shades of red, yellow and cream. These can rise up to 60cm above the foliage and appear throughout the summer.

Phygelius likes a warm spot in the garden, but with moist fertile soil in the summer. Deadhead flowering stems by cutting back to half their length to encourage side shoots and further flower stems for the autumn. All varieties will sucker from the base, particularly if a frost has cut them back, and they can be grown as herbaceous perennials in cooler areas. They are all hardy to –5°C and *P. capensis* will survive the occasional low of –10°C.

Capsid bugs can damage the new shoots in May, and they are susceptible to honey fungus.

P. capensis (AGM) produces yellow-throated orange-red flowers and '**Coccineus**' has scarlet blooms. *P. aequalis* '**Yellow Trumpet**' has attractive lemon flowers and only grows to 1m. There are many coloured types in the hybrid *P. x rectus*, including the popular '**African Queen**' with pale red flowers. '**Ivory Twist**' is the new white form. My favourite is the new dwarf variety '**Funfair Wine**' with magenta flowers.

Phygelius

Rosemarinus

Rosemary

This herb grows so well in the light, sandy soils of the islands that it is frequently used as a decorative plant in public gardens. Whilst it has many uses as a culinary herb, it certainly has its place in the shrub border too, with evergreen foliage and tiny pale blue flowers in spring and summer.

Rosemarinus is from rocky or scrubland sites in the Mediterranean, and has characteristic narrow rolled leaves and tubular flowers borne in whorls along the tips of new shoots over the summer. *R. officinalis* will withstand temperatures to –10°C, and probably more in a well-drained sheltered spot. There are numerous cultivars available in all different shapes, sizes and colours, both of the flowers and foliage. Some are hardier than others.

All do best in a hot sunny area with quite sharp drainage, as they don't like sitting in cold wet soil over the winter. They can be kept in shape by light pruning after flowering. As they age, stems can become woody, and they are susceptible to honey fungus, although little else affects them.

'Miss Jessopp's Upright' (syn. **'Fastigiatus'** and **'Pyramidalis'**) (AGM) grows as an upright bush to around 1.5m tall and wide with mid-blue flowers and a superb flavour for cooking. The long stems, stripped of the leaves, make great barbecue skewers, imparting subtle flavour to the food. **'Tuscan Blue'** is similar in form, with dark blue flowers. Both are hardy to –10°C with good drainage.

The **'Prostratus'** (syn. **'Repens'**) group is low-growing, to 30cm, and looks good tumbling over a wall, but it is less hardy, only coping with temperatures down to –5°C on rare occasions. There is even a variety *R. officinalis* **'Alderney'** but it is not one that I have been able to find locally.

There are some big Rosemary bushes used to good landscaping effect in the Esplanade car park in St Helier, Jersey.

Rosemarinus blooming in February

Whilst it has not been possible to include all the exotic shrubs that will grow happily in the Channel Islands, here are just a few others that I have seen over-winter with ease in local gardens.

Abutilon megapotamicum

This is a slender evergreen with arching shoots and bell shaped yellow and red flowers, originally from Brazil. It can be trained against a wall or fence, with support, or left as a shrub, growing to height and spread of 2m. It is hardy to –6°C.

The delicate flowers of *Abutilon megapotamicum* (AGM)

Cycas revoluta
Sago Palm

A cycad species that originated in Japan, it is best suited to very dry or stony locations in the garden. It produces whorls of leathery pinnate leaves on very slow growing trunks that eventually reach 2m. It can be grown in a pot for several years and is very drought tolerant. It is hardy to –4°C as long as it is in very well-drained soil.

Cycas revoluta (AGM) in Candie Gardens, Guernsey

Elegia

A member of the Restionaceae family that makes up a large part of the 'fynbos' region of South Africa. All 'restios' are strongly architectural and becoming more popular. They need acidic soil that is moist but free-draining and will grow to 2m given adequate water. Their elegant spires of fine leaves, like large horse-tails, make neat (non-invasive) clumps and they are hardy to –8°C.

Elegia species in a gravel garden, Guernsey

Leucadendron

There are various *Leucadendron* species, one of the many South African plants in the Protea family. They produce small, cone-like flowers that are surrounded by brightly coloured bracts in the spring and summer. They are best grown against sunny sheltered walls as they are marginally hardy to around –5°C only. Whilst *Leucadendron* is reasonably drought tolerant, it will grow faster if it is given adequate moisture. They grow to 2m tall. The closely related *Leucospermum* could be tried in similar locations.

Leucadendron in bloom in June

Melianthus major
Honey Bush

This evergreen shrub from South Africa has large toothed blue-green leaves and tall spikes of brick red flowers in late spring. These flowers can grow to an impressive 3m tall. In cooler areas, below around –4°C, the leaves die back and reshoot from the roots in the spring, like a herbaceous perennial.

The toothed blue-green leaves on *Melianthus major*

Sophora tetraptera

This evergreen shrub is known as the Kowhai in its native New Zealand. It has long pinnate leaves with around 20 pairs of dark green leaflets. It produces pendulous yellow flowers in late winter. Locally they are seen as large shrubs, around 2m tall, although they will grow much larger in New Zealand. They are hardy to –7°C, but appreciate a warm sheltered spot in well-drained soil.

Sophora tetraptera (AGM)

Also, despite some conservative temperature tolerances suggesting that the plants will not survive below 10°C, I have seen examples of *Lantana camara* and *Strelitzia reginae* that have come through several recent winters, in sheltered local gardens, to flower well during the summer. In very mild winters, many *Pelargonium*, especially the ivy-leaved and 'Regal' types, survive the winter also.

Various Cannas in Coronation Park, Jersey

Bulbs, Tubers and Rhizomes

There is a tale that the first Amaryllis bulbs were washed up on our shores from a shipwreck and were then collected by 'wreckers'. However, it is more likely that enthusiastic plant hunters brought them back from South Africa when the possession of exotic plants was something of a status symbol in aristocratic circles. All the plants in this section originated from southern Africa.

Pink form of *Crinum* x *powellii*

Amaryllis belladonna

Jersey Lily

This is, perhaps, Jersey's most famous flower, due to its association with Lillie Langtry, a Jersey born (1852) socialite, and one time mistress of the Prince of Wales. The nickname was popularised by a portrait of her entitled **'A Jersey Lily'**, painted by Sir John Everett Millais in 1878. However, Lillie is holding a Guernsey Lily (*Nerine sarniensis*) in the painting rather than a Jersey Lily, as no Jersey lilies were available at the time of the sittings. She was also sketched later by Frank Miles with a genuine Jersey Lily in her hair.

Amaryllis belladonna is also known as the 'Naked Lady' flower because it produces flowers in September, long after the leaves have wilted away in the spring.

Jersey has a long history of seafaring, with many islanders travelling as far as Canada to catch cod, then sailing on to the Cape of South Africa, where they would purchase exotic plants and return to Jersey with their goods. Many other native African plants (such as *Agapanthus* and *Lampranthus*) came to Jersey in this way.

The profits from such ventures allowed many Jersey families to build so-called 'Cod Houses' – large country houses, usually facing south in large gardens. Jersey Lilies thrived in the hot dry locations at the base of the granite walls and this is still the best planting location for these summer heat-loving bulbs.

The large bulbs are best planted with the neck just below the surface, in a hot and sunny spot. They prefer poor soil that is well-drained, and will flower better if overcrowded to an extent. The green strap-like leaves appear in April, dying back in early summer when the bulbs go dormant. In early September, tall (40cm) purple stems appear, topped with 4-6 pale pink trumpets that open in succession over a period of weeks. Although pale pink is the common colour, white and dark pink cultivars are sometimes seen. They are widely planted in gardens throughout Jersey in particular.

The bulbs are hardy to –7°C and survive without mulching locally. In colder areas a thick layer of mulch will give protection, or the bulbs can be lifted and stored in damp peat or sand out of the cold. Once established, *A. belladonna* doesn't need any special attention. If clumps do not flower freely, they are usually in too rich a soil, or the bulbs have been planted too deeply.

Right: *Amaryllis belladonna* with leafless purple stems, in September

Below: *Amaryllis belladonna*, The 'Jersey Lily'

Nerine sarniensis

Guernsey Lily

The *Nerine* genus contains the species that has been 'adopted' by Guernsey as their national flower. The 'Guernsey Lily', *Nerine sarniensis*, along with all other nerines, is one of the best late-flowering bulbs for the warmer garden.

Nerines are perennial bulbs that are widespread in southern Africa, especially in grassland where there is summer rainfall. A Guernsey legend suggests that the first bulbs were washed ashore on the west coast of Guernsey from a Dutch ship wrecked whilst 'en route' from Japan. However, they probably arrived in the Island as a garden plant via France in the mid-1600s.

All Nerines have narrow strap-like leaves that usually appear at the same time as the flowers. Up to 20 delicate, lily-shaped flowers develop in a sphere on a thin 45cm tall stem in the autumn. All the flowers have prominent stamens and wavy-edged petals in a variety of colours.

Their native habitat is mountainous scree slopes and grassland in southern Africa, and Nerines grow best in very well drained soil. Like the Jersey Lily, they do well planted against a house wall where the roof will afford some protection from the wet during the winter. However, flowering can be delayed by a dry summer and they appreciate some water as they come out of dormancy in September. It is important that the neck of the bulb receives adequate heat and sunlight so do not plant it in shade or too deeply. In cold climates, use a thick winter mulch as frost protection. Established clumps can be divided during the summer dormancy, but Nerines flower better if congested.

There are some 22 species of *Nerine*, (divided into three categories: summer-growing, winter-growing, and evergreen). The Guernsey Lily, *N. sarniensis*, is a glasshouse or conservatory variety in most locations, only hardy to −3°C.

Glasshouses in Guernsey are still known as 'vineries' from the time when they grew table grapes for the UK market and the Island continues to have an important cut flower industry. Nerine flowers were amongst the first cut blooms to be exported to London well over two hundred years ago. In later years, *Ixia, Sparaxis, Gladioli, Narcissus*, and then *Freesia* were exported, and, most recently, roses and carnations. Nerines are still grown outside in Guernsey gardens, and also in small commercial glasshouses for the local cut flower market. Autumn flowering *N. sarniensis* has 10-20 flowers per stem with an iridescent sheen over the bright orange-red petals. It is also seen in other colours. It is a stunning flower with a good vase-life and a chocolate-like scent.

The summer growing *Nerine bowdenii* (AGM) is the only reliably hardy species in the UK. It produces soft green leaves in the spring that often die off over the summer. It then produces a flower stem up to 60cm tall with a cluster of 7-10 pale pink trumpet-shaped flowers at the top in October. It is hardy to −15°C if kept dry over the winter. It is frequently mis-sold as the Guernsey Lily in many garden centres.

Left: *Nerine bowdenii* fill a border in October, Rozel, Jersey

Below: *Nerine sarniensis*

Zantedeschia aethiopica

Arum Lily

Although often called the Arum Lily, it is neither an arum nor a lily. However, it is familiar to most people, and certainly to florists, as the elegant white flowers that grace many bridal bouquets. Many people are unaware that it also makes a superb foliage plant, and is hardy enough to grow well in the Channel Islands. Originally from South Africa, where it grows alongside streams and lakes, it needs a warm position, in rich, moist soil that does not dry out in the summer. All *Zantedeschia* need full sun for at least part of the day, as they won't flower in deep shade.

It will reward a careful choice of planting site with bright green triangular leaves, up to 50cm length, and white spathes on 25cm tall stems from late spring on into the summer. The central spadix is creamy yellow, and the flowers have a vase life of over a week. Locally, the leaves remain green over the winter; in colder climates they die back and emerge from the rhizome in the spring.

This tuberous rhizome can be protected with a deep winter mulch, or planted in a pot and brought out for the summer months. If necessary, the rhizome can be lifted and divided at the start of the growing season.

Zantedeschia aethiopica (AGM) is the hardiest Arum Lily, down to –7°C and lower if the crown is under water. The variety '**Green Goddess**' (AGM) has unusual green spathes with white centres.

'**Crowborough**', with short white spathes, is especially hardy, to –10°C. They are a popular plant for damp gardens, and seen in many streamside plantings locally.

Other species, such as *Z. rehmannii* (AGM) with pink, and other coloured, spathes are not hardy and usually sold as the houseplant Calla Lily.

Zantedeschia aethiopica '**Crowborough**'

Other Bulbs, Tubers Corms and Rhizomes

All these perennials from the southern hemisphere and the Caribbean are well adapted to winter dormancy in our mild climate, with spectacular flower shows from mid-summer through into our warm autumns.

Canna

Canna Lily

Cannas are native to tropical America and the Caribbean, but were introduced in the late 1800s into other regions of the world and there are now innumerable hybrids across the various species. They are rhizomatous perennials, unrelated to the lily family although their large blowsy flowers are similar. Their other common name (Indian Shot Plant) refers to the small black seeds that resemble lead shot pellets.

They are grown for their large paddle-like leaves that can be up to 60cm long with fine veining, often in differing colours, and for their tropically coloured flowers. Each flower stalk produces several buds, opening in sequence up the stem over a period of several weeks during the summer and often into October locally.

Most varieties can be grouped under *Canna* x *generalis*, with erect flowers that are 7-12cm wide, in typically hot colours like red and yellow, but also in orange, pink, cream and bi-coloured forms. *C. iridifolia* has pendant pinkish-red flowers up to 11cm across whilst *C. indica* produces smaller orange flowers, 5-7cm across.

The fleshy stalks vary from 60cm right up to 2 metres or more, depending on variety and leaf colour varies from pale green, through yellow (*C.* '**Striata**') and red (*C.* '**Durban**') to the deep purple of *C.* '**Wyoming**'. *Canna musifolia* is a real giant

Canna indica

at 2.5m, resembling a banana plant.

Cannas flower best in full sunlight, but will flower in light shade. Although they tolerate dryish conditions, they grow taller with the more water they get, and appreciate a high potassium feed (e.g. a liquid tomato fertiliser) when in flower. They also grow well in a pot for several years. In ideal conditions the underground rhizomes spread rapidly, especially if they are left in the ground each year.

All Canna rhizomes will tolerate −3°C for the odd night as long as the soil does not freeze. Locally, many are left in the ground over winter. An extra couple of degrees frost protection will be afforded by mulching the crown. Cut down the stalks when frost has blackened the foliage, usually by December in the Islands. If over-crowding is a problem it is best to lift the clump at this stage, divide as you would a dahlia, and replant in the spring.

Cannas are popular as summer bedding 'dot' plants in public garden displays and are common throughout the Islands.

Right: The wonderful leaves of *Canna* '**Striata**'
Below: *Canna* '**Durban**' leaf

Crinum x powellii

Crinum x *powellii* (AGM) is the offspring of two less hardy *Crinum* parents from South Africa. It is a deciduous bulbous perennial with a massive fleshy stem and long blade-like leaves.

In late summer, clusters of large buds appear on tall stems. These open in succession over a period of several weeks to reveal fragrant, trumpet-shaped flowers in white and pink shades. The leaves begin to die down at this point, and are best cut away to leave the magnificent purple stems, rising up to 1.2m, on view, although they will need support on windy sites. Full sun is preferred and, once established, the huge bulbs resent being moved.

They do not need the poor soil that *Amaryllis belladonna* requires, but flower production will suffer if they are well fed. They are hardy to −10°C.

Pink form of Crinum x *powellii*

Crinum x *powellii*
'Album'

Crocosmia

Montbretia

Crocosmia is a cormous perennial from South Africa that is seeing a revival in popularity now that less invasive and more colourful cultivars are available. It is ideal for spicing up the late summer border with tropical coloured flowers.

Crocosmia have bright green, ribbed, sword-shaped leaves, 60-90cm long, and wiry flower stems that appear above the foliage in late summer. Each stem has a number of funnel-shaped blooms borne in two rows on branched stems. The old-fashioned Montbretia (*Crocosmia* x *crocosmiiflora*) has pale orange blooms and is a robust and rather invasive variety, hardy to –12°C. It spreads by corm offsets and by underground rhizomes and can be difficult to eradicate. It has even naturalized in some areas of the island. More tame varieties include the bright red '**Lucifer**' (AGM) and '**Emberglow**', the yellow '**George Davison**' and deep orange '**Emily McKenzie**'.

All *Crocosmia* prefer rich, moisture retentive but free-draining soil and full sun, although they will grow in partial shade. In frost-prone areas it is best to plant near a wall as many of the newer cultivars tolerate temperatures down to –5°C only.

Many examples are found in the public gardens of all the Islands where they are a popular landscape plant.

An elegant star-like bloom of *Crocosmia*

Eucomis autumnalis
Pineapple Flower

This bulbous perennial from South Africa has floppy strap-like pale green leaves up to 45cm long. In late summer, 20cm spikes bear a cylinder of numerous greenish-white flowers topped with a tuft of short green bracts. They are not scented, but are very unusual looking.

Eucomis are best grown at the foot of a sunny wall in gritty soil, and also do well in a pot. They appreciate occasional watering in the summer. *E. autumnalis* (AGM) and *E. bicolor* (with purple-edged petals) are hardy to −10°C and do not need lifting locally. They are easily propagated by seed and bulbils.

Eucomis autumnalis in flower in August, author's garden

Hedychium spp.
Ginger Lilies

Hedychium '**Pink Hybrid**' in front of *Musa basjoo* and *Canna*, author's garden

These are becoming more popular as they are spectacularly exotic in form and scent and are hardier than many people realise. *Hedychium* species are rhizomatous perennials from moist woodland in Asia and are closely related to *Zingiber officinale*, the root ginger used as a food spice and *Cucuma longa* from which we get turmeric, another spice. They have lance-shaped leaves on reed-like stems. Each stem produces a cylindrical spike composed of numerous tubular flowers with prominent stamens. Many have a wonderful scent that is usually more pronounced at night.

In their native habitat they need plenty of water during the growing season and are best grown in a part of the garden that retains soil moisture during the summer, in light shade if necessary. Flowering is better in full sun but this can compromise the growth if they are short of water. Established clumps flower more freely as long as they are not planted too deeply. Retain the leafy stems after flowering until the frost blackens them, to build up root reserves for the following year, before cutting them to the ground. Mulch acts as frost protection in the winter and as a water conservation method during the summer.

Red spider mite can be a problem in a dry summer, minimised by misting the plants regularly, but otherwise, they are problem free. The taller varieties will need support in a windy location.

Hedychium gardnerianum (Kahili Ginger) (AGM) is the easiest species to grow, with many coloured varieties. It grows to 2m tall and produces loose cylinders of yellow to orange flowers in late summer. It is hardy to –6°C. *H. gardnerianum* likes plenty of summer water but will cope without it. '**Pink Hybrid**' is a scented variety that has salmon flowers in late September. *H. coccineum* '**Tara**' (AGM) and *H. densiflorum* '**Stephen**' are other good varieties to try locally.

Mirabilis jalapa
Marvel of Peru

A bushy perennial from South America, seen naturalised in the Islands back in the 1950s. It was probably killed by subsequent hard winters, as the root only tolerates – 5°C. It has scented cerise, yellow, white or striped flowers, 5cm wide, that open in the late afternoon and close by the following morning, but flower over a long period in the summer. The leaves are pale green, and it grows to 60cm tall by 50cm wide.

Easily grown from seed, and flowering in the first year, it develops a long black tuberous root that can be lifted and stored over the winter in areas colder than the Channel Islands. It tolerates dry soils once established and can grow in full sun or light shade.

Pink form of *Mirabilis jalapa*

Acid Lovers

Whilst these are not especially 'exotic', they are such an intrinsic part of our local landscape that I felt it would be an omission not to include a few words about them in this book.

Rhododendrons at La Seigneurie, Sark

Camellia

Formal double-flowered *Camellia japonica*

The Channel Islands are renowned for this mainstay of our local winter gardens. Our acidic soils, ample rainfall and mild winter climate allow hundreds of Camellia varieties to flourish, particularly in many wooded valley gardens.

The glossy evergreen leaves and bright flowers, in shades of white, pink and red, make a cheery sight on cold February days and a good backdrop to emerging daffodils.

Camellias originate in Asia and the Far East. They come in a variety of heights, from 1 to 20m tall, and all have deep green lance-shaped leaves. Numerous hybrid forms, with single, double and anemone flower types are available, and all flower over the winter to early spring period.

All camellias are suited to moist, but well-drained soils in light shade. They do not flower well in heavy shade. It is important that the soil does not dry out in the summer as this prevents bud formation for the following season.

Camellias have shallow, fibrous roots that adapt well to container growing, and transplant easily provided they are watered well. They tolerate quite heavy pruning right after flowering.

They are prone to damage from vine weevils that notch the leaves in the spring, aphids and scale insects, and can also be affected by honey fungus. Pale leaves can be a result of iron deficiency, or alkaline soil.

Camellia japonica is the common species locally, fully hardy to –15°C. *C. sasanqua* cultivars are becoming popular as they flower around Christmas time and are also fully hardy.

February and March are the best times to see a wide range of camellias in bloom all around the Islands.

Rhododendron

Rhododendron bloom

This is a huge genus of shrubs from China and the Far East. They grow well in the Islands because of the acidic soils and reasonable rainfall. Like the camellias, the large blooms provide a welcome splash of colour throughout the spring. The commonly seen evergreen rhododendrons and azaleas are hardy to at least –10°C, and often –15°C.

Rhododendrons vary from small-leafed rockery plants, often known as azaleas, to vast tree-like specimens up to 20m tall. Bloom colour is more varied than the camellias with white, pink, yellow, orange, purple and red flowers, ranging from 3cm wide to a huge 30cm across.

Rhododendrons enjoy the humus-rich soil found in many local wooded valleys where they are also sheltered from cold drying winds. Rhododendrons are prone to a number of pests and diseases, including the common local problems of vine weevil and honey fungus.

It is impossible to recommend any particular varieties for local conditions, as there are just so many that are suitable. There are several specialist books on this genus and local nurseries will be able to suggest varieties suited to your particular requirements.

Pieris

Pink-flushed young
growth on *Pieris* in April

This is my favourite acidic soil plant because it has all year round interest. *Pieris* are natives of Himalayan hillsides and Far Eastern forests and enjoy moist soils and light shade like the previous two genera in this section. They will also grow in full sun if not allowed to dry out.

Pieris species are slow-growing evergreens with lance-shaped dark green leaves. The spring flowers begin developing in the autumn and the long panicles of buds, often red in colour, provide interest over the winter.

In the spring the buds open into long stems of tiny bell-like white flowers; it is sometimes known as Lily of the Valley shrub. Following this, newly emerging leaves put on a show of their own with pale green, cream and pink-tinted glossy leaves in sprays held above the existing leaves. It is not usually necessary to prune *Pieris*, but old flowers can be cut back immediately after flowering in the spring.

Pieris are generally pest free, but may suffer from *Phytophthora* root rot.

There are several species with many cultivars now available. *P.* **'Forest Flame'** (AGM) is one of the most popular varieties. It has bright red young leaves that become cream before turning green. It is hardy to –10°C. Most of the Islands' public parks and gardens have several varieties of *Pieris*, best seen in March or April.

Glossary

AGM: Royal Horticultural Society Award of Garden Merit. Plant does well in the garden, within its appropriate temperature etc tolerances.

Annual: Plant that completes its life cycle in one growing season.

Apex: Tip or growing point of a plant.

Biannual: Twice a year (pruning).

Biennial: Plant that completes its life cycle in two years, flowering in the 2nd year.

Bract: Modified leaf at the base of a flower, sometimes brightly coloured.

Bulb: Modified underground bud with fleshy scale leaves or leaf bases.

Calyx, (pl. calyces): Collective name for sepals.

Chlorotic, chlorosis: Loss of green colour (chlorophyll) due to mineral deficiency, low light or disease.

Cloche: Glass or plastic structure for cold weather protection.

Corm: Underground storage organ, replaced annually.

Corolla: Collective name for petals.

Corona: A crown-like growth on a flower, between the petals and the stamens.

Cultivar: Plant raised in cultivation that retains its distinct characteristics when propagated.

Deciduous: Shedding leaves annually at the end of the growing season.

Elliptic: Wide at the centre, tapering towards each end.

Evergreen: Retaining leaves for more than one growing season.

Family: Primary category in plant classification, including genera that have characteristics that group them together.

Genus, (pl. genera): Category in plant classification encompassing species that share characteristics.

Herbaceous: Non-woody plant that loses top-growth and becomes dormant in autumn, with growth resuming in spring.

Humus: Decomposed organic material, may include garden compost and leaf mould.

Hybrid: Offspring of genetically distinct parents.

Monocarpic: Plants that flower once and then die.

Monocotyledon, (Monocot): Flowering plant with a single seed leaf, parallel-veined leaves and flower parts usually in threes.

Panicle: Branched group of stalked flowers.

Perennial: Plant that lives for more than 2 growing seasons.

Petal: Modified leaf that forms the flower corolla, usually brightly coloured.

Pinnate: A leaf with leaflets either side of a central stem.

Radiation frost: occurs on clear, calm nights when temperatures near the ground drop below 0°C.

Rain shadow: An area having relatively little rainfall due to the effect of a barrier (e.g. house wall).

Rhizome: Horizontal branching fleshy stem growing underground.

RHS: Royal Horticultural Society, Britain's gardening charity, established in 1804.

Rosette: Dense circular arrangement of leaves arising from the crown of a plant at ground level.

Scandent: Plant that climbs over supports with flexible stems.

Sepal: One part of the calyx, usually green and smaller than the petals.

Spadix: Fleshy stalk embedded with tiny stalk-less flowers.

Spathe: Single outer 'petal', which is actually a bract.

Species: Basic category in plant classification consisting of similar plants that breed true in the wild.

spp. Abbreviation for several species.

Specimen plant: Ornamental plant grown in a solitary position, to be viewed from all sides.

Subspecies (abbrev. ssp.): Category in plant classification below species.

Stigma: Tip of female part of flower.

syn. Synonymous with, the same as.

Top dressing: Application of fertilisers to the soil surface around plants.

Tuber: Swollen root or underground stem.

Umbel: Flat or round topped group of many stalked flowers.

Variety: Naturally occurring variant of a species.

USDA: United States Department of Agriculture.

Conversion factors

°F to °C	Subtract 32 from °F and then divide by 1.8
Feet to Metres	Multiply by 0.3048
Miles to Kilometres	Multiply by 1.609347
Inches to Centimetres	Multiply by 2.54

Places to Visit

The Channel Islands have a wealth of public and private gardens simply overflowing with exotic plants. The local garden centres can supply many of these and are always happy to give advice on planting schemes.

PUBLIC GARDENS (all free entry)

Jersey
• Churchill Park, St Brelade's Bay (sheltered respite from the beach opposite)
• Coronation Park, Millbrook (great areas for the children while you wander round the plants!)
• Howard Davis Park, St Helier (my favourite, masses of exotica!)
• La Collette Gardens, St Helier (wonderful sea views)
• Parade Gardens, St Helier (superb exotic summer bedding schemes)
• The Esplanades at Gorey and St Aubin's Bay have plenty of palms and other unusual plants.

Guernsey
•Candie Gardens, St Peter Port
(a preserved Victorian pleasure garden, with exotic plant species and original 19th-century glass houses)
• Saumarez Park, Castel (run by the State's Parks and Gardens department).
• Sausmarez Manor, St Martin (also home to the rather wild Tropical Garden and Art Park in the grounds of this historic stately home. The manor and art park charge for entry)

Herm
Herm is run as a private enterprise and has developed its collection of exotic plants in recent years. It is well worth a visit from neighbouring Guernsey.

PRIVATE GARDENS
Jersey and Guernsey run 'Open Garden' schemes, whereby private gardens are opened up to the public on specified afternoons, usually for a small donation to charity. These larger Islands also have 'Floral Weeks' each year as a celebration of their floral splendour. There has also been success in 'Britain in Bloom' for some of the Islands' parishes.

Jersey
• Open Gardens from April to September (information from local garden centres and Jersey Tourism)
• Jersey Gardening Club (Tel. 854184)

Guernsey
• Open Gardens from April to September (information from local garden centres and Guernsey Information Centre)
• National Council for the Conservation of Plants and Gardens, Guernsey Branch. See www.nccpg.com for events
• Floral Week: Held at various times each year

Alderney
• Wildlife Festival takes place for a week in the spring, usually at the end of May. There is another festival weekend at the end of August.

Sark
• La Seigneurie (lovely walled gardens, free entry to RHS members)
• Wild Flower Fortnight takes place at the end of April.
• Guided Garden Walks take place throughout the summer.

Herm
• Guided Floral Walks run throughout the summer, by arrangement with one of the island's team of dedicated gardeners. See www.herm-island.com

ATTRACTIONS

There are several other sites of interest in the Islands. Some of those below make a charge for some, or all, of the amenities and visits may be 'by appointment' only. Tourism website addresses are also given.

Jersey
• Official Jersey website: www.jersey.com
• Durrell Wildlife Preservation Trust (the Zoo), Trinity. Superb landscaped grounds with a lot of exotic plants (and some pretty great wildlife too!) www.durrellwildlife.org
• Cooke's Roses, St Lawrence. www.cookesrosefarm.co.uk
• The Lavender Farm, St Brelade. Holds a National Collection of *Lavendula* together with a working lavender oil distillery set in landscaped grounds. www.jerseylavender.co.uk
• Lion Park, St Lawrence. Home to Flying Brands, postal pack flower business, landscaped gardens with boating pond and children's amenities.
• Samares Manor, St Clement. Lovely herb garden amongst other plantings.
• Sunset Nursery, St Ouen. www.sunsetnurseries.com
• The Eric Young Orchid Foundation www.ericyoungorchidfoundation.co.uk
• National Collection of *Cordyline australis*. www.holme-grown.com, Grouville
• National Collection of Alnus. Jersey Association Of the Men of the Trees. e-mail mottrees@jerseymail.co.uk

Guernsey
• Official Guernsey websites: www.visitguernsey.com, www.floralguernsey.gg
• Bruce Russell & Son, Gold and Silversmith, St. Saviour, has a large colourful garden, with water features.
• Castle Cornet, St Peter Port (Four period gardens including one restored by TV gardener Peter Thoday)
• Guernsey Freesia Centre, Vale
• Hauteville House, St Peter Port (Former home of Victor Hugo, small gardens)
• The Herb Garden at Auberge du Val Hotel, St Saviour
• National Collection of *Clematis* R J Evison Ltd, St Sampson 01481 245942
• National Collection of *Hebe* Mr M Searle, St Saviour 01481 263144

Alderney
• Official website, www.alderney.net or www.alderney.gov.gg (same site) Interesting natural history site: www.flora.org.gg

Sark
• Official website: www.sark.info

Herm
• Official website: www.herm-island.com

GARDEN CENTRES

For such small islands, we have a variety of garden centres and nurseries, well stocked with plants that do well in our climate. Many also sell pre-packed favourites such as *Agapanthus*, the Jersey Lily (*Amaryllis*) and Guernsey Lily (*Nerine*) for visitors to take home.

Jersey
Belles Fleurs Nursery, St Clement
Garden Scene Nursery, St Lawrence
Longueville Nursery, St Saviour
Ransom's Garden Centre, St Martin
St Peter's Garden Centre, St Peter

Guernsey
Earlswood Nurseries, Vale
Guernsey Gardens, La Ramee
Le Friquet Plant Centre, Castel
Martel's Garden World, St Andrew
Queux Patio Plants, Castel

Alderney
Alderney Gardens
Longis Bay Garden Centre

Channel Islands Climate Statistics

I am grateful to Frank Le Blancq and the Jersey Meteorological Office, Tim Lillington and the Guernsey Meteorological Office and Brian Bonnard in Alderney for the provision of the climate data.

1. Mean Daily Maximum Air Temperature (°C)

	Jersey (Maison St Louis) 1977-2006	Guernsey (Airport) 1977-2006	Alderney (Various locations) 1987-2006
January	8.5	8.5	9.1
February	8.7	8.2	8.9
March	11.2	9.9	10.1
April	13.3	11.5	11.5
May	16.9	14.7	14.3
June	19.5	17.2	16.8
July	21.6	19.4	18.5
August	21.9	19.7	19.2
September	19.7	17.9	17.9
October	16.0	15.1	15.2
November	12.0	11.7	12.1
December	9.6	9.7	10.1
Year	**14.9**	**13.6**	**13.6**

2. Mean Daily Maximum Air Temperature (°C)

	Jersey (Maison St Louis) 1977-2006	Guernsey (Airport) 1977-2006	Alderney (Various locations) 1987-2006
January	4.2	4.8	6.8
February	4.0	4.5	6.4
March	5.6	5.5	7.1
April	6.8	6.4	7.9
May	9.6	9.0	10.3
June	12.1	11.4	12.6
July	14.2	13.5	14.7
August	14.6	13.9	14.5
September	13.2	12.9	14.6
October	10.9	10.9	12.6
November	7.6	8.0	9.7
December	5.4	6.1	7.8
Year	**9.0**	**8.9**	**10.4**

3. Highest Air Temperature Recorded (°C)

	Jersey (Maison St Louis) 1894-2006		Guernsey (Airport) 1947-2006		Alderney (Various locations) 1851-2006	
January	14.3	1948	13.3	1948	15.0	1988
February	16.2	1948	15.0	1948	15.3	1990
March	21.1	1965	19.4	1965	17.7	1999
April	26.2	1984	24.3	2003	20.5	1994
May	28.9	2003	25.9	2003	24.9	2002
June	32.9	1976	30.8	1976	29.9	1998
July	34.8	1952	31.7	1952	28.4	1996
August	36.0	2003	34.3	2003	29.4	1975
September	33.3	1961	30.6	1961	27.2	1961
October	24.4	1959	23.3	1959	23.5	1990
November	17.6	1899, 1999	16.8	1999	18.0	1989, 1992
December	15.9	1953	15.6	1953	21.0	1992
Year	**36.0**	**2003**	**34.4**	**2003**	**29.9**	**1998**

4. Lowest Air Temperature Recorded (°C)

	Jersey (Maison St Louis) 1894-2006		Guernsey (Airport) 1947-2006		Alderney (Various locations) 1851-2006	
January	–10.3	1894	–7.8	1963	–9.0	1987
February	–9.5	1895	–7.2	1948, 1991	–6.0	1991
March	–3.5	1935	–2.2	1958	–2.8	1958
April	–3.0	1911	–1.4	1986	0.0	1970, 1975
May	1.3	1979	0.1	1979	0.0	1979
June	5.0	1962	5.4	1975	5.0	1975
July	8.7	1907, 1938	8.3	1954	7.5	1989
August	7.8	1960	9.2	1986	6.7	1993
September	6.0	1915	5.8	1974	6.1	1974
October	1.8	1997	3.5	2003	3.9	1964, 1967
November	–2.4	1915	0.0	Several	–1.1	1978
December	–7.2	1938	–3.8	1963	–4.4	1870
Year	**–10.3**	**1894**	**–7.8**	**1963**	**–9.0**	**1987**

5. Mean Grass Minimum Temperature (°C)

	Jersey (Maison St Louis) 1971-2000	Guernsey (Airport) 1977-2006
January	1.5	2.5
February	1.0	2.3
March	2.0	3.0
April	3.1	3.6
May	6.3	6.3
June	8.8	8.8
July	10.9	11.0
August	11.0	11.1
September	9.2	9.7
October	6.9	8.1
November	4.0	5.2
December	2.7	3.8
Year	**5.6**	**6.3**

(Grass temperatures are not recorded in Alderney)

Index

Illustrations are in **bold**

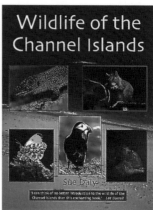